Leading
Change

UNIVERSIT

6832 Convent Blvd.
Sylvania, OH 43560

For Ruth, Charlotte, Callum, Cameron and Ashleigh (as always)

Leading Change

How successful leaders approach change management

Paul Lawrence

KoganPage

LONDON PHILADELPHIA NEW DELHI

First published in Great Britain and the United States in 2015 by Kogan Page Limited

Apart from any fair dealing for the purposes of research or private study, or criticism or review, as permitted under the Copyright, Designs and Patents Act 1988, this publication may only be reproduced, stored or transmitted, in any form or by any means, with the prior permission in writing of the publishers, or in the case of reprographic reproduction in accordance with the terms and licences issued by the CLA. Enquiries concerning reproduction outside these terms should be sent to the publishers at the undermentioned addresses:

2nd Floor, 45 Gee Street	1518 Walnut Street, Suite 1100	4737/23 Ansari Road
London EC1V 3RS	Philadelphia PA 19102	Daryaganj
United Kingdom	USA	New Delhi 110002
		India

www.koganpage.com

© Paul Lawrence 2015

The right of Paul Lawrence to be identified as the author of this work has been asserted by him in accordance with the Copyright, Designs and Patents Act 1988.

ISBN   978 0 7494 7168 2
E-ISBN   978 0 7494 7169 9

British Library Cataloguing-in-Publication Data

A CIP record for this book is available from the British Library.

Library of Congress Cataloging-in-Publication Data

Lawrence, Paul R., 1956-
  Leading change: How Successful Leaders Approach Change Management / Paul Lawrence. –
1st Edition.
     pages cm
  ISBN 978-0-7494-7168-2 (pbk.) – ISBN 978-0-7494-7169-9 (eISBN)   1. Organizational change.
2. Organizational behavior. 3. Leadership. 4. Management. I. Title.
  HD58.8.L384 2014
  658.4'092–dc23
                                                                                          2014039525

Typeset by Amnet Systems
Print production managed by Jellyfish
Printed and bound by CPI Group (UK) Ltd, Croydon CR0 4YY

CONTENTS

ACKNOWLEDGEMENTS

Whenever I compare anything I've experienced to giving birth, my wife becomes quite irate and assures me I have never experienced anything in the world as painful. I must acknowledge her perspective and cheerfully accept that there are some things in this world I will never fully understand. But I like the metaphor anyway. The ideas in this book have emerged from having spoken to, listened to and read the writings of so many different people I can't hope to recognize all the various contributors. At times I have felt almost overwhelmed, attempting to connect in my mind what different people have said and written and lay it all out in a way that makes sense. This truly feels like the outcome of a million minds, all squeezed through the rather limited funnel of my own capacity to comprehend and distil. Accepting that I can't possibly acknowledge everyone who has contributed to the writing of this book, let me at least acknowledge those of whom I am most aware.

First the storytellers. I knew some of the people who contributed to this book before I started; others I was introduced to along the way. Time and again I felt like a small kid sitting in a very big chair, listening to people talk with passion, integrity and emotion about some of the biggest events in their working lives. People, even those I met for the first time, trusted me with stories they would never wish to see appear in print. I'm very grateful for their trust, and for receiving permission to include the stories I have transcribed. I'm also utterly respectful of those who declined to see their stories included. I thank all the storytellers for taking the time to share their wisdom with me.

Next I'd like to thank three people who reviewed every chapter as it was written, sharing their experiences of reading the book and pointing out where my thinking appeared skewed. I'd like to thank Ann Ewing, Ann Whyte and Kieran White. Ann Ewing was my manager about 15 years ago when she was Vice-President for Organizational Capability for one of the biggest companies in the world. Ann Whyte is the Managing Director of WhyteCo, a coaching organization. Kieran White is my fellow Director at the Centre for Systemic Change (CSC). They each volunteered to read the book in addition to everything else they have going on in their busy lives, and I am very grateful.

Then there are the fellow practitioners and clients with whom I've worked over the years. I know for sure every one of them has shaped my perspectives in one way or another. I started writing a list, but the list got too long. I would like to mention Karen Hailwood, however, who provides me with coaching from time to time and refuses to let me pay for it.

I'd like to thank all of the people I've coached over the last five to six years. I've heard some people define coaching in terms of knowledge transfer, a process in which knowledge transfers from coach to coachee. In my experience coaching is a much more equitable relationship and I have learnt an enormous amount from all the people I've worked with. Perhaps the most extreme example of this happened a few years ago when Karen asked me to coach her on her fitness and wellbeing. While my coaching spectacularly failed to contribute to changes in Karen's life style, I was so inspired by her stories that I signed up to a gym on the spot, and have exercised five times a week ever since.

I'd like to thank my family. They have put up with me spending far too much of my weekend time over the last year working on this volume. My interactions with my children provide me with an ongoing reminder as to my own shortcomings when it comes to engaging in effective dialogue, and to the dangers of over-privileging the influence of positional power.

Finally thanks to the folks at Kogan Page who have worked hard with me to come up with a version of the book that will hopefully help you in your journey of making sense of change.

Introduction

We are apparently pretty hopeless at managing change, and we're not getting any better. Burnes (2011) listed a long series of change studies and meta-studies conducted over the last 40 years, all of which reported failure rates of between 60 and 90 per cent. The most commonly cited number seems to be 70 per cent. It's unlikely these numbers will surprise you given the plethora of books, articles and academic journals that begin by citing such statistics.

One of the most influential writers on change is John Kotter. In his classic 1995 *Harvard Business Review* article 'Leading change: Why transformation efforts fail' he described his own experiences of corporate change. He said: 'A few of these corporate change efforts have been very successful. A few have been utter failures. Most fall somewhere in between, with a distinct tilt toward the lower end of the scale', an analysis consistent with the failure rates outlined by Burnes. Kotter then went on to detail an eight-step process which, if followed, should greatly enhance the organization's capacity to implement change successfully.

Since the article was originally published many similar methodologies have been published in business books and magazines, designed by consultants and built into MBA syllabuses around the world. Just about every organizational development (OD) manager, and many business leaders, have heard of Kotter or are familiar with equivalent models and techniques. The business community generally is pretty conversant with this language of change to the extent that when I was seeking participants for this study several people looked at me quizzically and asked me if I didn't think enough books had been written about change already.

How is it then, nearly 15 years after Kotter's original paper, a McKinsey global survey claims that some two-thirds of change initiatives are still failing? People like me are still writing books and articles that start by declaring that 70 per cent of change efforts fail. Why aren't we getting better at change? Is it proving difficult to engage the broader organization with the value of the 'new' approach? Or is it that these change models are difficult to implement? Or is it that these models are actually no more effective than the approaches that preceded them? What is going on?

If 70 per cent of change efforts have been consistently failing, then 30 per cent have been succeeding. What can we learn from the success of the 30 per cent? Rather than explore why change efforts fail I set out to talk to people who have led successful change programmes, either business leaders or specialist change practitioners who work closely with such leaders. From what I learnt I came to the conclusion that the time may have come for us all, collectively, to undertake a great big 'paradigm shift', a shift that some of us have been contemplating for quite some time but that many of us are reluctant to commit to. The old paradigm is comfortable and reassuring because it offers the prospect of control and certainty. The new one provokes anxiety because it doesn't.

Old paradigm models are linear, implying that change can be achieved by following a sequential series of clearly defined steps. They appeal to those of us charged with committing to deliver specific objectives within a clearly defined time frame. Less appealing are the views of those who suggest we are kidding ourselves. Stacey (2012), for example, says that the idea that we can control outcomes by means of a sequential process of analysis, planning and execution is unrealistic. Stacey wasn't the first to suggest this. As long ago as 1990 Mintzberg suggested something similar. He said there are four conditions that need to be met if centrally planned approaches to driving change are to be effective:

1 One brain can handle all the relevant information.
2 That brain has detailed knowledge of every aspect of the situation.
3 The situation is relatively stable.
4 The organization can cope with a centrally articulated strategy.

If these conditions are not met, centrally planned approaches are likely to fail. Yet how many of those organizations that today rely on linear sequential approaches to change are operating in a simple, stable environment?

A surfing metaphor may serve to illustrate the point. If a surfer attempted to plan his every move before entering the water, and stuck to the plan no matter what, then he would fall off the board in no time at all; it's impossible to predict with precision the various impacts of weather, tide, shape of the ocean floor, movements of other surfers, etc. Instead, the surfer has to respond to changes in the environment as they occur, in the moment. In the new paradigm of change the change leader is the surfer, entering the water with a pretty good idea of what he wants to achieve, but uncertain as to how he will achieve it. To succeed he must become one with the organization and the environment, feel the shift in tides, the transitory change in currents and manage any sudden gusts of wind. As film director James Cameron is quoted as saying, 'To convince people to back your idea, you've got to sell it to yourself and know when it's the moment. Sometimes that means waiting. It's like surfing. You don't create energy, you just harvest energy already out there.'

The idea that the route to a desired outcome cannot be charted precisely in advance doesn't sit well with many organizations. The effective leader in the corporate world is the one who delivers, who neither under- nor over-promises, but can be relied on to get the job done on time. There is little tolerance for uncertainty or ambiguity and little room in this discourse for surfing metaphors. This creates a real challenge for those required to deliver change.

The purpose of the research on which this book is based was to find out how successful leaders and change practitioners go about their business. Do they deploy sequential linear methodologies despite the views of people like Stacey and Mintzberg? If not, then how are they managing and can we somehow distil the essence of their wisdom into something clear and tangible?

In Chapter 1 of this book I outline the research methodology in more detail and tell the story as to how the emerging change model (ECM) emerged. Parts I to III of the book explore the model in more detail, bringing it to life through the stories I heard, and relating aspects of the model to the work of other writers and researchers. Part IV pays special attention to some of the themes emerging from the ECM, themes that often show up in the change literature, such as leader authenticity, resistance to change and systems thinking.

The ECM provides a perspective on how change happens regardless and clues as to how the effective change leader might choose to intervene in that process. It doesn't provide a sequenced series of steps which, if followed, will assure the success of a change programme or initiative. This immediately sounds too vague and woolly for many of the people I meet upon my travels, and so although I feel I have little to offer to those who remain committed to finding a sure-fire formula for success, I recognize that others would appreciate some direction as to how they can get started working with the ideas outlined here. Part V of the book therefore provides some practical guidance. Chapter 13 is a case study. In Chapters 14 to 17 I then provide some general thoughts on how to get a change initiative started and consider some specific implications for leadership and building organizational capability.

Before we get going, a quick word on language. I didn't want to be writing 'he/she' all over the place, and so have alternated using 'he' and 'she' from chapter to chapter. I also struggled with the use of 'I' and 'we'. Where I'm talking about specific events, such as conducting an interview for example, I use 'I'. Where I'm talking about coming to a conclusion or drawing an insight, then I am more likely to use 'we'. This reflects a conviction that however personal it might have felt when I came up with an idea or experienced an 'ah-ha!' moment, these insights were a consequence of having engaged in dialogue with one of the storytellers, a client, or one of the colleagues I talk to every day. The writing of this book was a process of co-creation and it would be entirely inconsistent with the underlying philosophy of the emerging change model to claim it for myself.

So with the groundwork done, let's get straight into the guts of the ECM.

The emerging change model

T he purpose of this chapter is to make transparent the qualitative research methodology on which this book is based. It also provides an initial high-level view of the emerging change model (ECM) and a more detailed guide to the rest of the book than is provided in the Introduction.

Method

The research methodology deployed is based on grounded theory (Corbin and Strauss, 1990). This is an approach in which data collection and data analysis are conducted in parallel, and in which the nature of the questions posed to participants changes as you proceed through the study. Accordingly my semi-structured questionnaire only had one standard question, which was along the lines of: 'I'd like you to share with me two stories, first the story of a change in which you were involved, which you feel went well. Second, if we have time, the story of a change which you didn't feel went so well.' I subsequently explored those aspects of the stories that emerged most often, checking to see which factors appeared peculiar to particular storytellers and which appeared to be more generally present. I conducted all the interviews myself, analysing the results in parallel with the interviews, testing my analysis with colleagues on a regular basis as I looked for patterns and variations.

The 'storytellers'

I interviewed 50 people, looking for people with experience of working in complex change scenarios. This raises the question – what is 'complex' change? As we will see, the safest answer to this question is probably to assume that all change is complex, yet on the other hand we may have an intuitive sense that some change scenarios are more complex than others. I didn't establish hard and fast criteria as such, but I did seek out people with experience of leading change in multinational/multicultural organizations, and/or people who led big projects with several layers of management involved. I also looked for people from a range of different backgrounds working in different markets, and from different kinds of organization, to be able to test whether the themes that emerged appeared to be general and not specific to certain contexts. To meet these criteria, I spoke to colleagues and identified an initial list of 39 people, 35 of whom agreed to participate in a 60- to 90-minute interview. I contacted the remaining 15 interviewees through the original group of 35. I conducted interviews face-to-face where possible, or else by telephone or Skype.

Although my only sampling criterion was that people had experience of working with change, out of curiosity I profiled the 50 interviewees after the research was complete. The profile that emerged was as follows:

- 70 per cent were male and 30 per cent female;
- 80 per cent were business leaders, 12 per cent internal change practitioners and 8 per cent external change consultants;
- of the 80 per cent business leaders, 62.5 per cent had CEO experience and 37.5 per cent had other senior leadership experience, such as a head of function or head of business;
- 80 per cent were working at the time for publicly listed companies, 10 per cent worked in government organizations, and 10 per cent worked for not-for-profits;
- 40 per cent were Australian, 36 per cent European, 14 per cent North American, 8 per cent African and 2 per cent Asian;
- 18 per cent narrated stories of change spanning multiple countries; 38 per cent told stories of change interventions in Australia, 21 per cent in Europe, 7 per cent in Asia, 5 per cent in the United States, 5 per cent in Africa, 4 per cent in the Middle East and 2 per cent in South America.

I needed people to feel comfortable providing a full account of their stories including any feelings and uncertainties they experienced during the events described, and to share aspects of the stories that they wouldn't necessarily want to see appear in print. Therefore I haven't named any of the people I spoke to or their organizations. I've also disguised aspects of the stories when asked to do so by the storytellers.

Results

Corbin and Strauss (1990) distinguish between 'concepts' and 'categories'. A concept is the basis unit of analysis. Over time higher-level concepts emerge, which become the categories, and from the relationships between the categories emerges the overall theory, in this case the emerging change model or ECM.

FIGURE 1.1 Concepts mentioned by the 50 storytellers

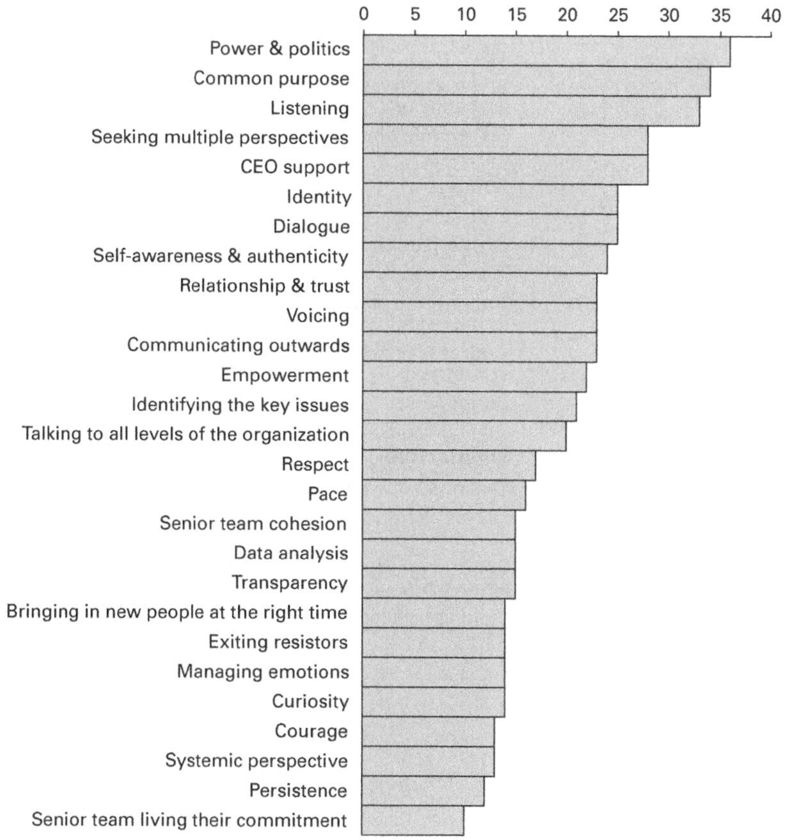

Concepts

Figure 1.1 shows all the concepts mentioned by at least 10 of the story-tellers. For example, 36 storytellers mentioned some aspect of power and politics in at least one of their stories, 33 mentioned the importance of a common purpose or direction, etc. I've presented this data for interest's sake only (remember I used a qualitative research methodology).

Categories

Figure 1.2 shows how I clustered concepts into categories. As the study progressed, so some of the concepts and categories shifted and changed. For example, dialogue emerged first as a category, but then became a sort of 'uber-category' as the connections between listening, voicing and reflection

FIGURE 1.2 Emerging categories

Dialogue
Listening
Dialogue
Relationships
Voicing
Language
Talking to all levels
of the organization
Reflection
Belief in people

Voicing
Voicing
Self-awareness/
authenticity
Communicating
outwards
Courage
Storytelling
Giving feedback
Transparency
Naming the elephant
in the room
Addressing others'
concerns
Simplifying

Identity
Self-awareness/
authenticity
Identity
Pace
Resistance to change
Leveraging resistance

Listening
Listening
Respect
Curiosity
Listening for meaning
Checking for
assumptions
Seeking feedback

Perspective
Talking to all levels
of the organization
Curiosity
Seeking multiple
perspective
Valuing outsider views

Power & politics
Power & politics
CEO support
Empowerment
Senior team cohesion
Senior team living their
commitment
Role of supervisors

Reflection
Curiosity
Self-awareness/
authenticity
Managing emotions
Learning through doing

Purpose
Common purpose
Identifying the key
issues
Burning platform

Systemic thinking
Identifying the key
issues
Data analysis
Standing on the
balcony
Bringing in new people
at the right time
Exiting 'resisters'
Systemic perspective
Persistence

became apparent. Some concepts first emerged as unitary, only to later become more multi-hued, such that they ended up connecting to more than one category. 'Self-awareness/authenticity', for example, ended up linked to three categories: 'reflection', 'voicing' and 'identity'.

The emerging change model (ECM)

The next step of the exercise was to identify how the different categories relate to each other. From that analysis emerged the ECM depicted in Figure 1.3. The model shows all of the categories except 'systemic thinking'. The model itself represents a systemic view, with reflective dialogue sitting within a context of constant ongoing change, and power and politics

FIGURE 1.3 The emerging change model (ECM)

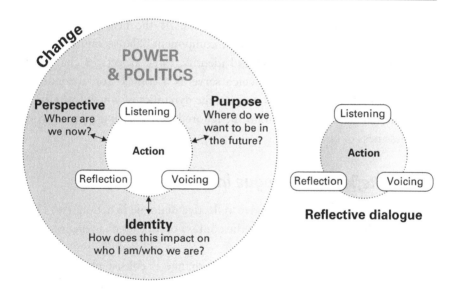

positioned as a backdrop. Some of the concepts listed beneath 'systemic thinking' are potential outcomes as a consequence of thinking systemically, for example 'bringing in new people at the right time' and 'exiting resistors'.

Exploring the ECM

You have probably already begun to make sense of the ECM. You may have attached meanings to words like 'listening', 'perspective' and 'identity' and at least partly decided what messages the model as a whole is intended to convey. I invite you to suspend those judgements for as long as you have an appetite for reading this book, and explore the extent to which the message I am trying to convey is consistent with what you are trying to hear. The change lexicon already includes words such as 'communication', 'listening' and 'politics' all of which, I have discovered through this process, lend themselves to multiple interpretations.

The model comprises three components. At the heart of change sits reflective dialogue in action, the first component. The second component comprises perspective, purpose and identity, three aspects of change that emerge through dialogue and which serve as a context for dialogue. The third component is power and politics, the dynamics of which form the setting for change and which cannot be ignored in navigating a path through the messiness of change.

Part I: Reflective dialogue in action

At the heart of the change we have 'reflective dialogue in action' (see Figure 1.4). This dialogue takes place in the context of an ever-changing organizational environment – 'change'.

Positioning dialogue at the heart of change is consistent with Stacey's (2012) notion of 'complex responsive processes' and the idea that change is a function of the interactions between people in an organization. Positioning dialogue at the heart of change is not a new idea. Isaacs (1999), for example, in part inspired by the work of Bohm (1996) wrote a marvellous book called *Dialogue and the Art of Thinking Together*. Kahane (2008) wrote an inspiring account of the power of dialogue in shaping outcomes in South Africa, Spain, Paraguay, Canada, Colombia and the Caribbean.

Part I of this book considers four aspects of reflective dialogue in action, each of which has its own chapter: communication and dialogue, listening, voicing, and reflection. I start by considering what we mean by dialogue and

FIGURE 1.4 Reflective dialogue in action

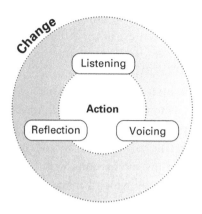

how 'dialogue' is different from 'communication'. Dialogue has two components to it: listening and voicing. The word 'communication' is ambiguous. It is defined as: the imparting *or* interchange of thoughts, opinions, or information by speech, writing, or signs (*Oxford English Dictionary*). In other words it can mean two-way communication, in which both parties listen and voice, or a one-way process in which one party is attempting to express as clearly as possible a particular perspective or point of view. This is a very big 'or'.

Many writings on change emphasize the importance of communication. 'You cannot over-communicate' and 'communicate-communicate-communicate' are familiar mantras. The emphasis however is usually on the one-way dissemination of information, rather than two-way exchange of perspectives. Kotter (1995) for example emphasizes how important it is for executives to 'use all existing communication channels to *broadcast* the vision'. Our findings support the idea that the clear articulation of the change message is necessary, but suggest it isn't sufficient. The focus on broadcasting or voicing hides the significance of effective listening, the importance of which is discussed in Chapter 3. To listen most effectively, the change leader enters into a dialogue deeply *curious* as to what others are thinking, and the basis for those perspectives. The change leader is willing and able to put aside her own perspectives for a moment and momentarily immerse herself in the point of view of another. The change leader who listens well is most likely to find that others respond well to her own voicing.

Chapter 4 considers effective voicing. Some people voice more effectively than others. At times of change most people in the organization want to know what's going on, but they don't just want to hear any old version of what's going on: they want to hear a version that is truthful and relevant, and that addresses their personal concerns. Through reflecting on the tales told by the storytellers in this book, I explore what differentiates an effective story from a less effective one. Why are some leaders regarded as trustworthy and credible and others are not? I differentiate between sincerity and authenticity and provide some insights as to what makes an effective change leader in this domain.

Effective dialogue is by its nature reflective. If I enter into a conversation genuinely curious as to what others are thinking and feeling, it means I am curious as to my own point of view as well, where that perspective comes from, and the extent to which it can adequately cater for any new insights I may gain from my interactions with others. Dialogue therefore implies reflection, a process by which I integrate what I've heard with my current reality, such that a new reality emerges. Reflective dialogue takes place around action. Change is an ongoing and dynamic process, and success cannot be assured solely through planning. The effective change leader *does* things, engages in reflective dialogue to make meaning of what happens as a consequence, and then *does* something else.

Part II: Perspective, purpose and identity

The second component of the model frames dialogue in the context of perspectives, purpose and identity. These are not just outcomes of dialogue; they also form the context for dialogue such that the relationship between dialogue and these other aspects of the model are best shown as two-way.

Perspective and purpose

Through effective dialogue we expand each other's perspectives. As an employee within an organization I only see bits of what goes on. I may feel passionately about my experience and may have come to some deep-rooted conclusions as to what my experiences signify. I can only engage in effective dialogue if I'm prepared to consider the possibility that my perspective is incomplete, and that I might think differently were I to gain access to a broader perspective.

Those who engage in effective dialogue are not only more likely to cultivate broader perspectives individually, but are also more likely to facilitate a broader shared perspective. Based on this common understanding of how things are *now*, people are more likely to form a common view as to how they'd like things to be in the *future* – a purpose.

FIGURE 1.5 The ECM expanded

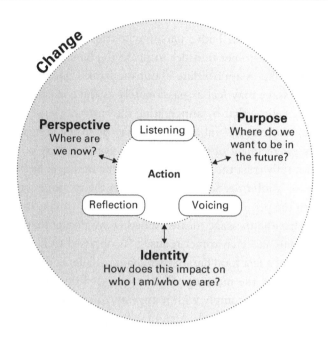

Identity

A common perspective on the present isn't sufficient to enable agreement on a common purpose. This is why all the data in the world aren't always going to persuade the organization to move in a particular direction. Through dialogue I also form and review my identity. This is a slightly more difficult concept to grasp, and is fully expounded in Chapter 8.

Essentially the point is that I have a sense of who I am in the world. I tell a story about myself, the kind of person I am, and how this shows up in how I behave in particular situations. For example, in my time working at a retail bank I came to understand how committed many branch staff were to their work. They saw a value in what they did, and derived satisfaction from helping other people manage their money more effectively, of being able to serve. These people had a work identity along the lines of: 'I am a person who helps others to succeed.' They worked in teams that had collective identities. For example, branches staffed by like-minded employees had a team identity something like: 'Our collective purpose is to help others to succeed through better management of their money.'

In this scenario staff may have felt truly threatened to be told they must now seize every opportunity to sell things to their customers – loans, insurance, pensions etc. This may have felt like being asked to inhabit a new identity along the lines of, 'I am a person who tries to sell as many products as possible to the customer in order to profit the bank.' This doesn't mean that there's anything inappropriate about the bank's intention. The person sending the message may feel as passionately as the branch staff, and may fundamentally believe that by anticipating the customer's needs and proactively meeting those needs unbidden, this may be in the best interest of the customer. As the recipient of the message however, this may not be clear, or else I may not fully trust the person who sent the message; he may just be a name to me, or a job title. So I will respond to the message by engaging in dialogue with the people around me to see what they think. Between us we will decide what the message means. Whether we decide that it means the bank is becoming more customer focused, as opposed to becoming an up-market version of a fast food hamburger chain, will depend on who I engage in the dialogue and the meaning we co-create. If I decide I don't like the new directive, but will comply with it anyway, this in turn will cause me to wonder who I really am at work. Again I will engage in dialogue with others and so aspects of my identity will change. This may happen at an individual level, team level or at the level of the organization as a whole.

Many change leaders voice frustration about how resistant others appear to be and label them as being 'resistant to change'. In fact resistance is entirely natural when considered in the context of identity. If I am asked to change my behaviour in a way that holds some significance for me, then I want to know how this new behaviour makes sense in the context of who I perceive myself to be, who I perceive my team to be, and who I perceive my organization to be. I seek to understand. It is the articulation of this questioning that is often labelled 'resistance' by change leaders anticipating unquestioning compliance. It's important to acknowledge the process through which people define themselves because identity is relevant to purpose. If the organization succeeds in achieving a common perspective on the present, it's likely there are multiple versions of future purpose. Identity is like a filter, a decision-making mechanism through which future options will be screened, but a filter that in itself may evolve and change through dialogue.

Part III: Power and politics

Some texts emphasize the importance of positional, or disciplinary power. This is the worldview in which the CEO's agenda and behaviours are most important. If the CEO is behind a change then the change will happen; if not, it won't. The importance of the CEO's support was affirmed by the stories. However, we also heard that just because the CEO supports the change, is even actively committed to change, that doesn't mean the change will happen; the story of power and politics is more complex than that. We also heard that the CEO can be one of the biggest potential blockers to change, one of the most powerful sources of resistance to change.

Some of the texts that emphasize the importance of dialogue and the primacy of co-creation seem to ignore power. This is the worldview that passionately ascribes to the famous Margaret Mead quote: 'Never doubt that a small group of thoughtful, committed people can change the world. Indeed, it is the only thing that ever has.' We did indeed find that dialogue sits at the heart of change, but that doesn't mean that engaging in effective dialogue alone is sufficient. As one of the storytellers said: 'Some people say all that matters is the conversation. No it's not.'

I attended a workshop recently that taught participants about collaboration. On one page of the workbook it said: 'For collaboration to work effectively, power games and politics need to be extinguished. Collaboration has nothing to do with power.' The ECM represents a view that says power and politics cannot be ignored or extinguished. The stories support the notion that there are many different sources of power available to people within an organization besides positional power. We have all heard of expert power, for example, or referent power. We go so far to say that there is a power imbalance in any relationship; indeed there may be several different types of power imbalance inherent in the same relationship, and these imbalances shift and change over time. Dialogue and power are related. I may enhance my power in a relationship through effective listening or powerful voicing. If I focus on discerning the nature of the power relationship between you and me during the course of a dialogue, then I am better able to craft my voicing as I go. So we have the whole model as depicted in Figure 1.3.

Part IV: Themes

Parts I–III of the book detail the ECM, with reference to stories and the writings of other authors. Some of the key themes of the model are discussed in Part IV of the book, namely:

- the significance of authenticity;
- what 'resistance to change' means; and
- systemic thinking.

Part V: Application

In the last part of the book we tackle the 'so what?' If the ECM isn't a linear process, how might we use it? In Chapter 13 I have written up a short case study to illustrate how the ECM may be useful as a reflective framework in practice. Chapter 14 is about getting started, with particular reference to getting clear on the purpose of change.

Chapter 15 considers the implications of the model for how we think about leadership. It is argued that leadership may be most usefully regarded as a mindset rather than a set of skills, a mindset that we may call 'fearless curiosity'. The fearlessly curious leader recognizes the world is complex, and that she will never have all the answers. She also recognizes that most other people regard the world as merely complicated and expect her to have all the answers. The fearlessly curious leader not only accepts that this as a dilemma, but relishes the ambiguity in all its mystery and sets out to navigate that complexity with relentless curiosity and fascination.

Chapter 16 provides some guidelines on how to go about building organizational capability from a systemic perspective. The traditional approach focuses on the development of the individual leader and her skills. I discuss some of the shortcomings of this approach and provide some general guidance on how to approach the task more systemically. In many organizations, adopting a systemic approach may prove challenging; the change manager may find herself therefore inhabiting a paradox (Shaw, 1997), trying on the one hand to fulfil a designated role within a culture that privileges accountability, control and certainty, while at the same time recognizing she is not actually in 'control' of anything.

Finally, in Chapter 17, I write specifically about the potential role of coaching as a particularly effective component of any systemic approach to building capability. I distinguish what I call 'systemic coaching' from other more conventional coaching philosophies. Systemic coaching is essentially the practice of reflective dialogue conducted with an awareness of the system outside of the individual coaching relationship.

The ECM as a reflective framework

Some models are built to be linear and causal, based on a premise that says people are generally resistant to change and cling to the status quo like limpets. The task of the change leader is to stir up the seas to such a degree that the limpets are shaken loose, before being moved swiftly on to a new location where they have the opportunity to reattach themselves to a new status quo. These models are inevitably linear, invoking some form of diagnostic early in the process, after which the emphasis turns to enrolment, implementation and a process of bedding down, of making change stick. This assumption is evident in some of the language used. Lewin's 'freeze – change – refreeze' model (1951), for example, appears to imply change as a discrete event taking place against a backdrop of stability and predictability. The task of the change leader is to establish the need for change and to put in place a plan by which everyone involved in the plan is informed of this need, and of the role they must play to make the change happen. These models imply that people at the top of an organization are ultimately responsible for identifying the need for change, the nature of the change, and for making sure that the desired change is implemented. The role of people further down the organization is to comply with the wishes of those further up the organization, or else to resist. Such models are alluring to those seeking certainty and control, but this isn't one of those models.

Other models are built to represent more complicated systems. In this case the relationships between variables may be less linear and outcomes less predictable. Nevertheless, it is implied that all variables are included and that the model may be expected to function reasonably well in helping the user predict outcomes. This isn't really one of those models either. This model assumes the world is complex rather than complicated. The essence of complexity is the multitude of variables that impact on our environment both in isolation and in combination with other variables in ways that are unpredictable and uncontrollable. The interaction of these variables creates a 'mess' through which the effective change leader must successfully navigate. The change leader is the surfer, reflecting on the consequences of her last action, continually adjusting to circumstance.

I don't claim that my analysis of the stories depicts every aspect of change. We bring our own experiences and beliefs to a study such as this, which heighten our awareness of some factors and may blind us to others. Given that I'm not attempting to represent every aspect of a complicated process, this doesn't matter. The potential value of the model lies in serving as a reflective framework to which the change leader can refer in the moment when making choices in navigating her own 'mess'. The model is an attempt to represent the combined reflections of 50 experienced change leaders, and through them the wisdom of the thousands of other people with whom those people have interacted over time. In that sense this model is a co-created hypothesis as to what some of the most important aspects of change might be.

The linear, sequential approach to change represents the old paradigm. Leaders who believe in the primacy of positional power and hierarchies often see their role as being to issue an edict to the wider organization through the filter of their direct reports. According to this model the leader's role is to tell the essentially passive organization, engaged in 'business as usual', what to do. Upon hearing the instruction the organization then embarks upon a quick flurry of activity whereby it changes what it's doing in accordance with the leader's wishes. Contrast this to the new paradigm which depicts the organization as being actively involved in change all the time, in which the organization is constantly assessing and re-assessing its actions with reference to everything going on around it. It isn't the role of leadership to instigate change *per se,* for change is ongoing. Rather it is the role of leaders to notice how change is already happening, and to pay attention and be mindful of the way in which they choose to attempt to influence the direction of that change.

The ECM is therefore best used as a reflective framework. As more people engage with the model, talk about the model, ask questions of it and offer their insights, so the model will continue to emerge; indeed it will never stop emerging. The emerging change model is not intended to generate a methodology that will lead to specific outcomes. Rather it is intended to provide useful insight to others reflecting on their practice: change leaders and change practitioners.

The reluctant practitioner

Working with a step-by-step process sounds much easier! Can't we just keep doing things the way we always have done? Well, we sort of can and we sort of can't. From the standpoint of the reluctant practitioner there's bad news and there's good news.

First the bad news. Stacey (2012) came up with a model that distinguished between different types of change, the idea being that the practitioner could tailor her approach to different change scenarios and use all the old models in many of those scenarios. Unfortunately he lived to regret it. The problem with such a model is that it assumes we can successfully diagnose in advance the extent to which a challenge is simple or complex. It implies that levels of complexity can be somehow gradated and represented on a spectrum, as if they were not complex at all but merely complicated. The best approach may be to treat every scenario as if it were complex. Higgs and Rowland (2005) compared multiple approaches to managing change and concluded 'complex' approaches tend to be the most effective regardless. Tsoukas and

Hatch (2001) suggest we simply assume that all change is complex. Complexity from this perspective is just a metaphor. If we treat all organizations as complex systems and view them accordingly, then we begin to see things we would otherwise miss or that we would attempt to frame within simple linear systems of cause and effect. The sense we got from the people we interviewed was that the behaviours they engage in, in managing complex change, appear to be based on a more general conviction as to how they can most effectively behave as change leaders. So that's the bad news; you can't ignore the principles that underpin the ECM.

The good news is that the ECM isn't a model for designing and implementing change; it's a model that attempts to depict how change happens anyway. In this sense it's an overlay to how the change practitioner goes about getting things done. So long as the practitioner doesn't expect that adherence to a linear model will get the job done without the need for further review, then I can see no harm in using whatever tool, model or process that feels useful. The ECM may be regarded as a framework or lens through which to review events as they unfold. This presumes the change leader is a reflective practitioner, and I think the reflective practitioner will enjoy experimenting with the ECM.

PART ONE
Reflective dialogue in action

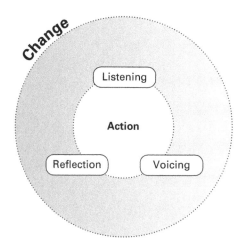

Dialogue and communication

Communicate, communicate, communicate?

In 2006 Laurie Lewis and colleagues obtained copies of the 100 best-selling books on organizational change as listed by Amazon.com and analysed those books to identify what were the most common pieces of advice (Lewis *et al*, 2006). Most of the books emphasized the importance of communication, usually with reference to sharing a vision or announcing that change was coming. Although a few books talked about participation, the predominant theme was leaders communicating clearly downwards so that as many people as possible knew what was going to happen and why. For example, Duck (1998) wrote:

> Communications must be a priority for every manager at every level of the company. It is important for the messages to be consistent, clear, and endlessly repeated. If there is a single rule of communication for leaders, it is this: when you are so sick of talking about something that you can hardly stand it, your message is finally starting to get through.

Larkin and Larkin (1994) suggest providing line supervisors with 3×5-inch laminated cards upon which are written the key points about a change to help them answer people's questions. The emphasis is on dissemination, pushing the message down, on managing the style and content of the message, and on planning the propagation of the message. Where participation is mentioned, often this appears to be more about creating a place for people to 'feel' more involved and to discuss the change in service of complying with it. Four of the 100 books reviewed by Lewis *et al* (2006) talked about making an example of those who don't comply. One even had a section called 'Enlist star power or have a public hanging'!

Forty-six per cent of the people I spoke to in the research also emphasized the importance of disseminating the message, for example the importance of:

> Communicating at all levels regularly. I started with my leadership team, then the whole organization. I needed to get my direct reports aligned and

functioning and working as a team, understanding that they were responsible and accountable for cascading it down. I did town halls and written communications; people were hungry for direction.

Other storytellers also talked about the importance of effective one-way communication. Here are three examples:

I 'over-communicated'. You need to keep repeating the message. People go into denial. They rationalize what they hear and take away a different message, particularly if the change is seen to be negative. You must keep the communication simple: First, what are we doing? Second, why are we doing it, and third, what does it mean to you? You need to be explicit and honest. I didn't have internal communications people and so I wrote it myself. People knew it came from me.

I had a very effective project management office. We shined the light on what was wrong, what was working and what wasn't. We knew what we needed to achieve and were relentless in issuing reports and holding people to account. We reported to an internal committee chaired by the CFO and encouraged frequent communication. That said we still got criticized for not communicating enough.

We met resistance for different reasons and at different levels. We managed the pushback by making it clear from the start that there was no wriggle room and communicating that regularly. That helped a lot. Previously local management said yes but then didn't really do it. In this programme the central team went out to the business to help them clearly define the plan and make sure they were sticking to it.

However, more than half the people I spoke to didn't make specific mention of the importance of communicating outwards. It may be that some didn't feel it was worth mentioning, that they took for granted it would be assumed they engaged in effective one-way communication, but few mentioned it as one of the two or three key success factors they believed contributed to the success of their project. More emphasis was placed on engaging people in the change process, for which merely repeating a message appears to be an inadequate strategy.

Communication, monologue and dialogue

The *Oxford English Dictionary* defines the word 'communicate' as to 'share *or* exchange information or ideas'. To share implies a one-way flow of information while to exchange explicitly defines a two-way flow. The emphasis in the change literature is on the sharing or dissemination of information rather than exchange. The Lewis *et al* article includes the word 'listen' just four times, without elaborating on its significance.

In contrast I heard the word 'listen' much more often; listening was mentioned by 66 per cent of the people I spoke to. The following story was recounted by an external practitioner contracted by a European organization to design and implement a new group leadership development strategy:

I spoke at a conference where I told the story of how we successfully implemented a global leadership programme in a huge multinational. I was approached by another international company to come and do the same for them. I hadn't been there long when people started asking me, 'What's taking so long? Couldn't you speed things up?' I told them I had a programme at home they could have, but I wasn't convinced it would work for them or if it was what they needed. When I contacted them, the operating companies told me that the team at the centre was always coming up with things then lobbing them at the operating companies where they were quickly put on a shelf. Things began to get tense.

I was assigned a bright, smart, German person to help me. She was a bit more forgiving but still said: 'I'm worried... when will we actually start doing it?' I told her that the content wasn't the issue, there's lots of content around; we needed to engage the organization and have them wanting it, whatever 'it' was. One day, the global Head of HR walked past as we were talking and asked me how things were going. The message she left us with was: 'clearer – faster – quicker!' Eventually, I persuaded her to give us time. My colleague also began to understand the approach we were taking, and started to talk in terms of what 'we' were trying to do – the project was now jointly owned. What took time was talking to loads of end customers in the businesses, about things that had been done before; what had worked and what hadn't. For example, the folks from a plant in Russia said: 'We can't have people off the line for long.' We heard things we couldn't ignore, and it became obvious that the process would be complicated; many of the messages were competing.

Then I physically left the safety of the 'mother-ship', the telephones and e-mails, and went out to speak with employees. We set up workshops with people from different levels of the organization all in the same room, at the same time. We talked to front-line leaders about what it was like to be a front-line leader in the presence of mid-level leaders and direct reports. We tested some of the things we'd heard and tested some of the ideas we had had. People really liked the sessions. In one session in Egypt they said: 'This is great! We should have more conversations like this.' In Nigeria people flew in from all over the country to be at the sessions. People got very interested and we learnt a huge amount.

When it came to designing the programme it looked very different to anything the company had done before and some people had to let go of that. However, once the programme was out there, the feedback was great, and the company began to see the initiative in a different light. There was a meeting of all the HR managers and apparently they said: 'This is the way we should be doing things from now on.' The businesses said they saw the centre working in partnership with them, that their views were being listened to, and that they saw how the design of the programme reflected their different perspectives.

When I choose to share my intentions with others with the expectation that they will understand and comply with those intentions, this is monologue; there is only one 'logic' at play. Had our storyteller taken his off-the-shelf programme and attempted to implement it across the new organization, selling its benefits and interpreting pushback as 'resistance', it is unlikely he would have been successful. Instead he determined to first understand the world through the perspectives of his end-users. If I'm seeking an exchange of ideas then this is dialogue; I'm inviting the other person to bring their logic to the interaction. The communication of change in many organizations however is monologic. The implicit message is 'This is what we have decided. Please do your bit in making sure it gets done' (Jabri *et al*, 2008).

Monologue as coercion

Schein suggests that the change leader who expects recipients of a one-way communiqué to comply with their message without question is engaged in 'coercive persuasion' (Stacey, 2012). No response is required; indeed any form of questioning is regarded as resistance. There are two aspects of 'coercive persuasion' worth highlighting here. First, coercive persuasion is often presented as an invitation to collaborate. The words and the style of delivery may suggest a desire for consensus and to hear all views, but the reality is different. This is monologue presented as dialogue.

I had personal and awkward experience of such a process early on in my corporate career when working for the European division of a multinational energy company. The head of the European business invited 500 people from all around the continent to a two-day conference, the objective of which was to settle on a strategy to take the business forward. He had read a management text which suggested that successful companies chose between one of three 'value disciplines' and stuck to that discipline (Treacy and Wiersma, 1996). He had shared the book with his executive team and asked them which of the three strategies they thought was most appropriate for the business. Between them they chose one of the three value disciplines before convening the meeting of the 500, the objective of which was to engage the wider business. I usually sit at the back of the room at large gatherings so that I can see everything that's going on, but on this occasion I arrived late, and ended up on the front row.

During the morning the senior team told the story of how they had chosen one of the three value disciplines and explained how they believed this would bestow upon the organization competitive advantage. Before lunch we were all asked to stand up, and then to sit down again if we agreed that this new approach would indeed deliver us a competitive advantage. In all innocence I remained standing, wondering how adopting this discipline would deliver us competitive advantage if our competitors were implicitly adopting the same discipline. Because I was sat (or rather standing) in the front row I failed to notice until it was too late that the other 499 people had all sat down. Feeling vulnerable I fielded a couple of questions from members of the senior executive, the heads of the country businesses, who stood around the perimeter of the room in various places. They asked me what it would take for me to sit down. The answer was – not much. I sat down as soon as I felt able to do so without looking foolish. Later that day one of the executive came up to commend me for my courage. He assured me that my actions hadn't constituted a career-limiting move, though it was just as well I sat down when I did. Around the tables at lunch and dinner the real meaning that people were making of the event emerged, and their authentic levels of commitment became clear. In reality many people were sceptical as to the likelihood that the different business units would commit to the initiative in practice, despite the declarations of commitment from the country heads. In the event the initiative lasted about a year until the head of the European business left the organization.

McClellan (2011) tells the story of an art college's attempt to redesign building spaces to accommodate increased student enrolment and promote environmental sustainability. The change process included collaborative workshops at which it was intended the different stakeholders would come together and agree a way forward. McClellan sat in on some of the workshops and found that change proposals supporting people's existing understanding of what the art college was, what it did, who it served (its identity) were generally supported. Those that challenged that identity were closed down. Consequently all of the agreed changes supported the existing identity of the organization and transformational change wasn't achieved. In other words, McClellan saw an absence of dialogue and the domination of monologue. People were focused on their own points of view and invested little energy in exploring other's ideas. No one was happy with the overall outcome of the process, which people came to regard as a non-productive talk-fest. McClellan argues that change often fails because those who manage it suppress the emergence of conflicting organizational meanings in service of driving forward a predetermined narrative.

To what extent are our own communications monologic or dialogic? Efforts to corral people around a particular point of view, to get people to sign up to a predefined outcome, are all monologic. It's common for change leaders to seek consensus by bringing large numbers of people together in a forum in which they are supposedly able to express their views in a frame that is nevertheless monologic (Jabri *et al*, 2008). There's even been a word invented for this kind of intervention – *facipulation*. Facipulation looks like facilitation, but in fact the facilitator is pre-committed to a particular point of view. The resulting 'consensus' is often skin-deep. In the absence of discord such events are often declared to be a success, and it is assumed that people are committed to the new way forward. In practice the absence of discord often doesn't mean consensus at all; instead it means that people have recognized the existence of a pre-defined outcome, and decided there's little to be gained in pushing back.

Dialogue happens anyway

An external practitioner tells the story of an organization hit hard by the global financial crisis (GFC):

> Everyone was downsizing and the management team knew the business was liable to fail. How to communicate? What to say? They were starting to not communicate and no one knew what was happening. We did an off-site and they were desperate. Panicking. It's important to realize that leaders get scared too, and when they do they stop communicating. They said they couldn't tell people, but what they didn't take into account is that people were talking anyway. If you can get the senior team talking to themselves then they feel more comfortable about sharing with others.

If we replace 'dialogue' with 'monologue' in the ECM, then:

- There is no sharing of perspectives ('this is how things are').
- There is no negotiation as to what the future might look like ('this is how things are going to be').

- There is no consideration of identity ('You must do it whether you believe it is the right thing to do or not').

- There is an assumption that change may be achieved through the exercising of positional power ('If I ask you to do something I expect you to do it').

To replace dialogue with monologue is actually meaningless. Change doesn't typically happen through monologue, and dialogue happens anyway. Just because the change leader chooses not to engage in dialogue doesn't deter others from engaging in it, and it is through that dialogue that change emerges. People engage in dialogue and they share perspectives. They discuss possible futures and they question those futures against the stories they tell about themselves, their teams and the organization. Dialogue takes place whether 'management' wants it to or not. In this context the suggestion by van Vuuren and Elving (2008) that organizations should try to 'limit the amount of informal communication as much as possible' seems curious. Change leaders decide whether they want to participate in dialogue or not. If they limit their contribution to monologue then others will engage in dialogue about that monologue and collectively decide how to respond. The change leader who distances himself from dialogue is likely to be surprised and disappointed with the change that emerges.

Johansson and Heide (2008) identified in the change literature an implicit assumption that the success of change efforts depends on the regular provision of clear information – about the nature of the change, the reason for the change and of the individual's role in the change process. In other words, keeping employees well informed is the key to success. Unfortunately, as the authors point out, people make their own sense out of what they hear, and are generally resistant to others making sense for them. The change leader who declines to engage in dialogue is in effect declining to participate in that sense-making process.

Getting out and about

To engage in dialogue means getting out and about and talking to people. Forty per cent of our storytellers spoke of the importance of engaging with others at all levels of the organization with an explicit intention to learn and understand. One of our storytellers was seeking to implement a new business model in an Australian retail organization, a change that impacted on every employee and a national network of franchisees. The programme of work was wide-scale and complex, and the execution of the programme was forecast to result in significant improvements to the company's bottom line, so there was considerable pressure to deliver the work on time. In this part of her story she talks about some of the things she did that were important in delivering the change successfully. I asked her what personal qualities she brought to the work, one of which was about dialogue:

> With one or two colleagues I explained the change to every retail business in each state and explained it personally. What and why. Authentically and open. It made me accessible so they could understand, and I gained an understanding of what their concerns were so I could hear and respond. Nothing beats regular face-to-face conversation versus an edict from head office delivered by e-mail, etc. Recognizing uncertainty makes it believable for people. It was my project manager's idea and it added an extra two weeks to the project timeline, but she convinced me and I recognized she was right afterwards. I had been tempted to do it quicker via e-mail.

One CEO calls it MBWA – 'management by walking about. I always cultivate touch-points in an organization, people who tell you stuff openly. I need to know. You need lots of people.'

One barrier for senior leaders is a belief that this is not what senior leaders do. Senior leaders, after all, need to prioritize. Spending time talking to staff further down the organization is time that would be best spent 'strategizing', or else it constitutes encroaching into the domain of managers in the organization. This is what one of our storytellers had to say about that:

> If I'm to be effective I need to be dynamically on the ground and involved. I keep getting told I'm too involved in the detail. HR keep telling me to let managers further down the organization come up with the answers themselves; but what if they don't know the answer? I need to be part of the conversation. I need to know when to intervene and when not. My direct reports and my direct reports' direct reports are always part of my communication. I've got to take a lot of people with me and I can't risk things getting lost in translation.

Another of our storytellers talked about habits learnt in transforming a business that was massively impacted by the GFC:

> Here I'll meet with eight people from the organization at a time and sit down for an hour of informal talk, each group comprising people from the same level in the organization. I'll share what's on my mind for five or ten minutes and use the rest of the time to find out what's going on. I understand some of the

managers don't like me doing this, I think because they feel a little threatened by it, so I do sessions with them too. That way I have another avenue to talk to everyone in the company. I also have an internal website that everyone has access to which enables anyone in the company to ask me a question anonymously. I always post both the question and answer and it enables fantastic two-way communication. I had someone pick me up on something I'd said at two consecutive town hall meetings, noticing that what I said the second time was inconsistent with what I said the first time. They were right! Some of the questions they ask are hard to answer, but it's a great way to engage. The response from staff has been overwhelmingly positive as everyone knows they have a voice.

For some people I spoke to this seemed to be an ingrained behaviour. Some looked at me strangely wondering why I seemed so interested, but not all leaders do engage in this way. For example, I recently spoke to a CEO about the value of talking to people at all levels of the organization. Her office was on the top floor of the building, a floor that was considerably emptier and quieter than any of the other floors in the building. As I talked about the value of engaging directly with others, she wrinkled her nose, before telling me she relied on others to do that for her. I interviewed another CEO about a change programme happening inside his organization, sponsored by him and managed by his OD manager. I interviewed him as part of a longitudinal piece of research aimed at understanding the impact of the change at all levels of the organization and in different locations of that organization. He said he didn't have a view as to what was going on in the organization below the level of his executive team. As CEO, he said, he felt cut off.

On several occasions over the years in my facilitator role I've suggested to senior leaders that they make an appearance at leadership workshops; to share the context for the programme and to engage in a dialogue with participants; to share perspectives on what's happening in the organization. I've seen leaders do this marvellously well; I've seen other leaders appear uncomfortable; and had some decline the invitation. These are examples of forums in which change leaders have the opportunity to engage relatively informally with their organizations, to learn as well as inform, but some leaders restrict their communication efforts to more formal events in which the emphasis is on voicing rather than listening.

Shaw (2002) calls these unofficial forums, at least those in which people feel safe to express their views, part of the 'shadow system'. The shadow system is the part of the organization that exists outside the 'coercive monologue'. The change leader who remains within the comfort zone of the monologue doesn't know how people are *actually* making meaning of the proposed change as opposed to how they are *intended* to make meaning. They don't know what people really think and feel. This doesn't matter much if the 'shadow system' is aligned with the formal system. If it is not so aligned however, the change leader soon finds himself disengaged from the actual process by which the organization defines itself. Shaw (1997) suggests that many change efforts fail because leaders fail to tap into these systems.

Beech *et al* (2011) use a different metaphor, that of Schön's 'swampy lowlands' (1991). They contrast the 'high ground', the tangible and knowable conceptualization of problems, with the swampy lowlands where problems are messy and confusing, and where resistance to change often manifests itself, bogging things down. This resistance is based on embedded assumptions, attributing the cause of failure to change to others, and participants failing to reflect upon their own role in events. An approach to change emphasizing the dissemination of a monologic message into the swampy lowlands is unlikely to lead to change. A more promising approach is to engage in reflective dialogue.

Barriers to dialogue

Engaging in dialogue may be hard for a leader if:

- The leader believes in hierarchy and the sanctity of positional power. For someone who believes that people should do as they are told, engaging in dialogue may seem like a waste of time. Why encourage people to explore possibilities when I've already decided what needs to happen next? What's the point in encouraging people to come up with ideas that I will only have to dissuade them from?
- The leader fears being asked difficult questions. This leads us to a consideration of authenticity, discussed in Chapter 10.
- The leader doesn't listen well. This leads us into the next chapter, Chapter 3.

These traits play out across the organization over time. If the leader believes in the value of hierarchy then in time the organization as a whole is likely to come to believe in hierarchy, and to depend on its leadership to come up with all the answers. Likewise if the leader fears being asked difficult questions, the organization will stop asking difficult questions, believing that open and transparent dialogue is unlikely to be welcomed.

To commit to dialogue means committing to being authentically curious; curious as to how others see things, how people are relating personally to the prospect of change. Dialogue is transformative. As Carl Jung (1933) said: 'The meeting of two personalities is like the contact of two chemical substances: if there is any reaction, both are transformed.'

To commit to monologue means committing to *not* listening or hearing, to focus on telling and expecting compliance. The problem with monologue in this context is that command and control approaches to change rarely work. The command and control approach assumes that the prescribed solution is the right solution, and this in turn assumes that a few people at the top of an organization are capable of determining the right solution to complex problems. The future leadership of an organization committed to monologue will have few options other than to work out the solution for themselves, since they have in effect committed to not listening.

KEY POINTS

- Most texts on change emphasize the importance of communicating outwards: the repeated dissemination of a clear message.

- The word 'communication' may also be used to mean two-way communication. Two-way communication that includes authentic listening may be described as 'dialogue'.

- Change leaders often seek engagement through monologue. This may lead to initial compliance, until such time that compliance presents a problem for the recipient of the message, when it is likely to lead to unexpected, often passive, resistance.

- To engage in dialogue requires genuine curiosity in other people's perspectives. This is particularly difficult for those who believe in positional power and hierarchy whose primary objective is agreement to a pre-defined outcome.

- Beware facipulation!

Listening

Sixty-six per cent of the people I spoke to made explicit reference to the importance of listening, much more often than shows up in other narratives around change. Michael Mauboussin, Chief Investment Strategist at a US global investment management firm, talking about managing complexity, said:

> Most managers, even executives, aren't naturally good at drawing out other's opinions… The key is to make sure that as a leader, you're not just tapping, you're actually almost extracting this unshared information from everybody and putting it onto the table to be evaluated. And that's where a lot of organizations fail. (Sullivan, 2011)

Some of our storytellers spoke about being constantly curious. For example, one CEO said: 'I know I don't have all the answers. The answers sit in the organization and I'm really keen to find out who has them and to bring them to bear.' Another talked about continually seeking out and reflecting upon other's insights:

> You need to communicate, communicate, communicate… and listen. The solution shouldn't be hard-wired. For example, we decided to outsource our call centres. Our frontline staff said, 'Have you really thought through what clients will think?' An account manager told us the reason one of our major clients did business with us was because he got to deal with us direct and not through an outsourced operation. It did get me thinking about how we would need to communicate it to clients and the rationale for doing so. I was grateful for the insights and recognized we had more work to do before pressing the button.

From our storytellers I heard that many leaders make concerted efforts to listen to the views of their broader organizations. For example, this is the story of a CEO who travelled the world as part of a global change programme, narrated by an external practitioner who worked with him closely on the programme:

> He and I travelled from South Africa to Mexico, to Argentina, Chile and Brazil, just to talk and listen. We collected information, as did other groups, collated it, and put it to a number of internal people, who put it to the executive team.

From that emerged four principles that accompanied the commercial goals. From this point on, because they owned it, people honoured it. Everyone knew they were on a journey and they had ownership all the way throughout the process because they felt listened to and because the CEO himself sat and listened.

This may sound obvious, but then we heard so many other stories in which the instigators of change didn't apparently listen. Again, we wonder if that may be because so much of the literature on change talks about 'communication' as if communication were a monologue, and because people often reach senior levels of organizations by being smart, adopting a leadership identity that includes being able to come up with solutions independently. Monologue may work when the task is complicated, but not when the task is complex, a distinction discussed fully in Chapter 12.

Different ways of listening

'Listening' is a word, like 'communication', that means different things to different people. People don't often talk about different *forms* of listening; instead they talk about the *extent* to which people listen – 'how *hard* were you listening?' It may be more helpful to discern between different forms of listening. In this context we can differentiate between listening for what we expect to hear, and being open to the possibility that others may have something to say that we haven't thought of.

Clutterbuck and Megginson (2005) cite a lengthy tract from the work of Williams (1965) who expresses this beautifully. Extracting an extract from an extract:

> The skills of the good listener... are indeed exceptionally necessary... but these are consciously different from the stance of the leader who is merely listening to the discussion to discover the terms on which he can get his own way.

One language that reflects the difference in the stories we heard is about agenda-full and agenda-less conversations. This storyteller was the CEO of a large Australian company:

> There's no substitute for going out and talking to people. It's a myth that the higher up the food chain, the busier you are. The reality is you should be less busy. You need to have time to talk to people, to think and to reflect. It's about getting out and about without an agenda. An agenda is a series of meetings. I go out with no other intention than to just talk to people and sound them out.

Others are afraid of that – 'Thank God my in-tray's full, now I don't have to be strategic.' You find out far more by getting out and talking to people than you do from a monthly report.

This storyteller gave an account of the behaviour of one of his direct reports:

> I think he had an innate sense of how to drive change. It didn't happen instantly; he made an effort to get out there and meet people, even had a baby in the middle of it. When he went out there it wasn't about going out with an agenda, or sending data; it was about listening. So they felt trusted and heard. It's a tough skill to teach people.

In contrast this storyteller recounted the efforts of a leader who was less successful in listening, despite travelling widely:

> He does come out and visit us from time to time, sometimes unannounced, but it's always about his agenda and what he's trying to achieve. He doesn't appear to be interested in what we have to say. When I do manage to get a word in and tell him about some of the problems we're having, that we need him to fix, he assures us that everything will be sorted out. But there's no follow up and it doesn't get sorted out. These issues have a serious impact on our business and he doesn't seem to care.

Listening to others through the filter of our own 'agenda' can lead to spectacular misunderstandings. We are all inherently quick to jump to conclusions and often feel encouraged by our environment to make a decision quickly based on the information available. Sometimes situations do demand rapid decision making. The problem, as expressed by Sargut and McGrath (2011) is that: 'Most executives believe they can take in and make sense of more information than research suggests they can.'

We are more likely to hear about people paying close attention to other's perspectives from those working cross-culturally. For example, westerners often warn each other that in Japan, 'yes' (in terms of the message sent) doesn't always seem to mean 'yes' (in terms of the message received). I heard a few stories about the need to listen differently when working cross-culturally. For example, this story was recounted by an engineering manager leading a team of westerners working in Russia:

> We were western engineers operating in a totally different environment. The key was going to their institution, their system, and accepting that we were in their 'house' even though we had the 'purse'. They were paid regardless of efficiency whereas we weren't. We had to find ways to get them to accommodate some of our requirements. Westerners who tried the authoritative approach got

blacklisted and had to leave. Patience, persistence and respect were required. We looked at things very differently, and we needed to understand how they thought and why.

However, we may not be so diligent when working in more familiar surrounds. Based on the discussion so far, consider this hypothetical exchange:

> *Manager*: 'I'd like to see you improve your communication skills' (intended meaning: I'd like to see you giving others more space in which to express themselves).
>
> *Report*: 'I'll get to work on that right away. Thank you for the feedback' (interpretation: You want me to speak up more often and not let others interrupt me).

If we don't check that we have fully understood the intended meaning of an utterance, then we assume a meaning, based usually on a projection of our own values and beliefs. The meaning we make can often be very different from the meaning intended.

Listening for the meaning

In busy environments, with a focus on getting the job done, these kinds of misunderstandings happen all the time. We have a built-in tendency to hear the words and attach our own meanings to those words. We don't check that we've understood the meaning behind the words. One of our storytellers talked about working with an executive who later became the CEO of a very large global multinational:

> He was someone who respected strength and took any apparent lack of confidence as a sign of weakness. It's a shame the relationship went the way it did because he could have learnt from me given that people were so terrified of him. I often arrived at meetings ahead of him and when he arrived the mood changed. People were on edge with him and so he only heard from the confident. I felt like saying to him: 'Listen to the spirit of what people are trying to say, not just the words.'

Another of our storytellers spoke of a personal insight into her own approach to listening, how she began to notice the extent to which she might be listening primarily through the lens of her own agenda:

> I've started noticing when I'm upset and how that's when I tend to be most critical of others. Most people turn up to work wanting to do a good job. I need to listen out for what they're trying to achieve as opposed to what I'm seeing them achieve.

Listen first

Effective listening supports effective voicing. Consider the difference between starting a new job and launching immediately into telling people what needs to be done, and stopping to hear what's really going on first. This storyteller was appointed CEO of a manufacturing/wholesale business whose products weren't selling for a number of reasons, including the removal of government subsidies. Before deciding on the vision for the business he spent months finding out more about the company and the industry within which it operated:

> The business was based in California with manufacturing sites all round the world. It had a massive cost structure and a massive revenue line. It was losing money and it was very complex; locked-in contracts, moving inventories, convoluted supply chains. It was always selling out of product but it wasn't selling enough, and the market had just turned down. When I was appointed I didn't know what to do. I visited the competition first. People asked me why I visited the competition before I visited our own factories – did it mean I thought they were useless? That I had decided already to sell the business? But I knew that China was up and coming and that none of my factory managers had been there. Visiting the competition first meant I knew what questions to ask of the people in my own factories; operators, shift supervisors – everyone. This helped me build up a picture. I spent a long time talking to people. At town halls people pulled me aside and told me what was happening. In one instance a factory manager asked me why the company had kept the factory open for so long. I asked him if he realized what the consequence would be for him if we closed it. He said – of course, but the factory shouldn't be here. It became obvious what to do and the big decisions emerged from the process. I bothered to listen. It sounds trite, but it's the fundamental bit. To get to that level of trust you need to have a genuine interest in their point of view. You can't fake it.

Contrast this story with the following account of another organization's response to crisis:

> The way the company responded to the crisis was a knee-jerk response. It was easy to understand; the commentators were saying 'the company is fundamentally flawed' and so they took a risk-averse response. Suddenly there was a desire to manage everything at a much lower level of detail, like a blanket. Some areas did require tighter management, but it was a classic over response to apply it everywhere. Declaring to *everyone* that we had problems *everywhere* led to a huge breakdown in trust. It's so important to find out why something

goes wrong. No one felt it was appropriate to challenge; it was taboo. People said, 'this is how we have to behave and respond.' It slowed things down and stifled intellectual debate. The only thing that was important was being able to demonstrate to external stakeholders 'we're fixing it'. It was one of the reasons I left.

As Covey (1989) put it: 'seek first to understand, then to be understood'.

Leaders' assumptions about leaders

Several of our storytellers talked about the assumptions people make about themselves as leaders, including an expectation that they shouldn't have to listen, that they should be able to work out the answer for themselves:

> I myself needed to go through a personal change journey. I needed to learn to shut up and listen. I had to be less aggressive. You get to leadership because you know the answers. You need to transition to asking questions, and it's not a transition everyone makes well. I recognized it was a journey that I needed to make.

This storyteller spoke about coming into an Eastern European organization as the new CEO. The business was in trouble and a new approach was required. The leadership team didn't know what to do, but didn't feel they could ask:

> The organization and indeed the country were very bureaucratic. I had a lovely session with the senior leaders about communication. They said they couldn't talk to the organization without having answers. I told them that the answers were in the organization – not in this room. I had to get the leadership team comfortable with not knowing the answers.

Authentic curiosity

It's hard to listen outside of our own view of the world without being authentically curious. This requires silencing our own judgements and channelling our energies into exploring what is going on for other people. If we listen from our own view of the world then we're likely to selectively hear what seems to best fit that view. Some of our storytellers talked about this with reference to respecting others. Thirty-four per cent of the people we spoke to talked about respect. For example one person said:

'What drives me? I have an unshakeable belief in the goodness of people. People deserve to be listened to. That is my life's pursuit.'

This next storyteller spoke about a CEO who succeeded in turning round an underperforming business in two years:

He did it by going and talking to everyone. He was very measured and unflappable. He went and talked to all the different stakeholders – listened to their rantings, waited until he understood what they wanted. He was genuinely humble and treated everyone with balance. He was the CEO and the buck stopped with him, but he talked with people eyeball to eyeball, with respect.

Another expression of this authentic curiosity we heard was about a personal commitment to learning:

The other day on a teleconference the CEO and executive were talking about the difference I had made, and they said that it's because of who I am as a human being. I didn't expect them to say that about me. I just have a deep interest in where people are coming from, while at the same time recognizing that everyone has a boundary that needs to be respected. I love the concept of the 'beginners mind', that every day is a learning day, taking everything as fresh, new and shiny. It's like that film 50 First Dates, treating every engagement as if it was the first.

People can be dismissive of the need to listen, defining listening solely in terms of being quiet while others speak. This may be because people don't consider the difference between listening from one's own agenda and listening from the other's agenda. Again, this difference is easiest to discern with reference to cross-cultural examples.

One of our storytellers related her personal experience of community members' attempts to improve road safety statistics in the Northern Territory of Australia. In the Northern Territory the number of deaths attributable to unsafe driving is three times the national average. Factors cited include not wearing seat belts, alcohol and fatigue. There are also local issues. While indigenous people make up 28 per cent of the population, they represent 50 per cent of road deaths. Many of those people live in remote communities and most haven't grown up with English as a first language. Educational campaigns have been rolled out in the Northern Territory in the local language, including song competitions, targeted road safety instruction, and workshops. Yet while such road safety campaigns may have been successful in other parts of the world, there has been no obvious downward trend in accidents in the Northern Territory.

Why wouldn't a standard road safety campaign, tailored to remote communities and delivered in the local language, succeed? The Ninti One organization, a not-for-profit company based in Alice Springs, conducted published research into unsafe driving practices in Ntaria, a remote community 130 km west of Alice. Talking to residents of the community they discovered that:

- The closest car repair facility to Ntaria is 130 km away.
- In the case of medical emergency people may have to travel long distances to the nearest hospital.
- There is no public transport.
- Driving instruction is primarily in English.
- Licensing and registration is organized from the local police station, but for various reasons people tend to avoid going to the police station.

They also explored further the 'bush mechanic' phenomenon. Fixing vehicles in innovative ways is a strong aspect of male culture in some aboriginal communities, with skills passed down the generations. The Australian Broadcasting Corporation (ABC) made a series of documentaries on bush mechanics in 2003. The series followed the adventures of a group of young Aboriginal men as they travel across the central desert in their dilapidated cars which are continually breaking down. Each time a car breaks down, they manage to fix it. In one scene, for example, the men mend the crack in a radiator. They take the lead from an old car battery, melt it in a hub-cap over a fire and pour it over the crack. They refill the radiator using fluid from the wind-screen wiper container – and off they go again. The Ninti One study discovered other innovative practices including the use of seat belts as tow-ropes and filling flat tyres with clothes.

An effective strategy for improving road safety statistics in Ntaria is unlikely to be achieved without being authentically curious as to how this community works. Yet our first approach is often to implement an approach that has worked elsewhere and, if it doesn't work, apportion blame to the individual, team or community perceived as resisting change. In this particular instance it appears unlikely that any improvement will be achieved without venturing into the community, agenda-less, curiosity-full. Yet how hard is it to put aside one's own assumptions, based on years of experience, and open one's mind to the idea that our world isn't the same as everyone else's world? Again, this shows up more clearly when considering cross-cultural examples. It is more difficult to recognize how fast we apply the same assumptions to situations that are not so obviously different; how quickly we assume the world operates within the confines of our own perspectives. How unwittingly, in our efforts to make the complex simple, we end up making the complex simplistic.

Listening to ourselves

Listening isn't just about listening to others, but also about listening to ourselves. Listening deeply, not only to what is being said but also for the assumptions and beliefs that appear to underpin what is being said, is not about listening to others in isolation; it is about listening to others while at the same time listening to ourselves. If we all had the same values, beliefs and expectations; if we all had similar life experiences, then we wouldn't need to be so curious as to what underlies the utterances of others. People are not different, full stop; they are different to us. People are not strange, full stop; they are strange relative to us. People are not eccentric, full stop; they are eccentric relative to us.

It is difficult to be curious if we hold to a view that there is a single correct way of doing, thinking and feeling: our way. From this perspective there is our way (the right way) and other ways (strange ways). It is difficult to be curious about others without being curious about ourselves. If we are not curious about ourselves, if we don't question our own assumptions and beliefs, then we are more likely to form quick judgements about the behaviours and attitudes of others. Recognizing yourself in an issue makes it easier to put aside your own judgements and to explore the world from the other person's perspective.

Seeking feedback

We've discussed respect and a commitment to learning as two characteristics of a good listener, someone who is authentically curious. A third characteristic is an unceasing ongoing request for feedback. Not many people ask for feedback. Jackman and Strober (2003) wrote a classic paper in which they described the oft unspoken fear of feedback that exists in many organizations. Subordinates are afraid to receive feedback because they are afraid to be criticized, for criticism is a form of monologue that threatens self-identity. To be criticized is to be threatened. The most common response to threat is defence. Managers therefore fear giving feedback because they are afraid that the person will either be stirred into a passionate, even angry defence of his behaviours, or else he will withdraw behind an unbreachable wall, or else he may have no defences and may break down and cry. None of these responses are likely to lead to an improved relationship. So in most organizations people tread carefully, to the extent that feedback may not happen at all, or is else limited to awkward annual performance review meetings and the ad-hoc use of anonymous 360-degree feedback.

For the curious listener however, feedback is gold. Frank and honest feedback informs; it helps add more detail to the picture. It helps the listener to become more self-aware, more able to explore an issue without being overly prejudiced by her own point of view. Sixteen per cent of our storytellers spoke about the importance of proactively seeking feedback. Three examples:

> I seek feedback continually. People think I'm weird, but in asking for feedback people recognize they have a voice and are respected.

> As a leader you're never off-duty and always on stage, so it's really important to have people who'll tell you the truth about how you show up. Leaders need to appoint people to do that. It's very easy and comfortable to isolate yourself when the going gets tough. Feedback is a crucial part of being effective and making a difference.

> I attribute part of my success to being resilient. You have to be prepared to persevere even when things don't go as you want. I actively seek feedback – being resilient means I can take it.

KEY POINTS

- We don't have a ready vocabulary to differentiate between various forms of listening.

- There is a fundamental difference between listening with an agenda and listening without an agenda.

- Listening without an agenda is hard. It entails recognizing the nature of our own agenda, including some of our own assumptions and beliefs that underlie that agenda, and putting aside the anxiety that others may not see things the way we see things.

- Some leaders don't seek to understand the views of others because they see it as their role to know all of the answers, and to disseminate those answers to people lower down the organization.

- Without listening there is no dialogue, and therefore no perspective sharing, no process through which to consider common purpose, and no opportunity to understand some of the personal and emotional issues that can show up as 'resistance to change'.

- To be prepared to listen requires a confidence and resilience borne of high levels of authenticity.

Voicing

04

All this talk of complexity and the senior executive's incapacity to work out the answers by themselves may lead some people to think – what is the role of the change leader then? Is it to sit back and watch change emerge regardless? Of course the answer is no. Change in complex situations may not be controllable, for there are too many variables at play, many of them operating beyond the awareness of any one individual, but people can and do influence the direction of change. The interventions people make may not have predictable outcomes, but they do have outcomes. The task of the change leader is to reflect on those outcomes and make new choices about how to most effectively intervene. The primary means by which leaders can intervene is by giving voice to what they are thinking and feeling.

Great expectations

Change is constant and for many people represents a threat. When things change people want to know what it means. Change represents a reduction in certainty, and people look for an interpretation of events that restores at least some of that certainty. People look to colleagues, to local management and to the leadership of the organization to provide that meaning and certainty. People certainly expect to hear from their leaders. People don't necessarily expect that what their leaders say will make sense; they do so in the hope that what their leaders say will contribute to their capacity to make sense for themselves. The sense-making process is social. What the leader says is only part of that process, but an essential part.

Chapter 3 included the story of the CEO of a manufacturing/wholesale business who spent months finding out more about the company and its industry before deciding what needed to happen. He talked about the fundamental importance of listening, and how what needed to happen emerged from the dialogue he engaged in with others. Later in the story he also talked about the importance of voicing:

> Once it became clear what we needed to do then I declared that we would make those changes. People were used to others coming and saying what needed to be done. They said they would do stuff then didn't follow it up. Lots of people

told me I would never do it, that the broader organization was afraid of losing volume and incurring big write-offs. They told me the organization wouldn't let it happen, but I had support from the top. I had been sharing my plans with the Board as they formed every three months.

During times of change people throughout the organization expect senior leaders to provide a perspective on what's happening. Leaders have 'declarative powers' (Tsoukas & Chia, 2002); the power to introduce a particular interpretation of events. If leaders forgo this responsibility then this may lead to a breakdown in trust (Judge & Douglas, 2009; Allen *et al*, 2007). Declaring a perspective doesn't mean people will immediately align around it; people will make their own meaning ultimately, but the leader is expected to have a view. The effective 'voicer' should not therefore always expect the outcome of a declaration to be compliance. Rather he should expect, and be listening for, the response to his declaration (Jabri, Adrian & Boje, 2008).

I have worked with two organizations recently that underwent wide-scale restructuring that went on for more than twelve months. In each case the change started from the top and worked its way down. In each case managers at all levels didn't know what the future held for them. The change was perceived to be coming from the CEO, whose direct reports didn't initially seem to know what was going on, or else felt unable to share what they knew. After a few months, in each case, the senior executive team was appointed. Then the senior executive team seemed to go into another long huddle with their direct reports again without communicating what was going on. By the time the restructure reached the lower levels of management they had endured more than a year of uncertainty, an experience that for many was both stressful and a source of disaffection and disengagement with their organization. The leadership of both organizations lost the trust of their people by staying quiet.

Although people throughout an organization clamour to hear the view of their leadership, this doesn't mean that they are prepared to accept whatever message is delivered. The message needs to make sense otherwise people will be just as disappointed and disengaged. On the face of it this may appear a formidable challenge, but herein lies the difference between monologue and dialogue. At some point a new direction must be established. If leaders have engaged in dialogue before coming to a conclusion, then it is much more likely the organization will engage with the message. If it is the view of the change leader, after having engaged in dialogue, that the right way forward will nevertheless feel unacceptable to many people in the organization, then at least the change leader will be able to frame the message in terms that will be most palatable, and to anticipate the response. For a message to make sense it must:

1 Resonate with the recipient's perspective on the world.

2 Be experienced as open and transparent, with nothing held back.

3 Be delivered with authenticity and sincerity.

Furthermore the change leader must come across as confident, willing and able to engage in further dialogue as the organization prepares for the next stage of change. These conditions loosely match four critical behaviours of change leaders identified by Higgs and Rowland (2010) upon interviewing 33 change leaders. They found that effective leaders create compelling stories that connect emotionally with the organization, tell it like it is and hold others to account, are self assured and able to create a safe space for dialogue, and publicly commit to an outcome demonstrating personal vulnerability if necessary.

1. Resonance

In the last chapter the importance of listening was emphasized. Too many change texts talk about the importance of communication as if it was monologic. Listening is important because leaders make better decisions when they listen to others and become informed.

In Chapter 2 I said that 46 per cent of the people I spoke to talked about the importance of communicating outwards in navigating change. Simplistically we can differentiate between two types of outward communication; informed and ill-informed. Change leaders who communicate a change agenda that is ill-informed don't do so intentionally. They may point to data, to the views of selected people in the organization, to industry experts etc ... They consider themselves to be informed, but if they are not inclined to listen to the people whose cooperation they seek, then they will be relatively ill-informed. Being informed isn't only about working out the right solution, it's also about knowing how best to communicate that solution to different audiences.

Generic communications, disseminated by e-mail or posted on websites, are rarely effective. Different people have different perspectives on the organization, different roles, different ambitions and different hopes and fears. Effective voicing addresses individual differences (Michaelis, Stegmaier & Sonntag, 2009), which means, logically, that the organization collectively needs to understand what those individual differences are and respond to them. The widespread communication of a change agenda must therefore be a collective effort, since no change leader has the time to engage every person in an organization individually. Unless it's a very small organization.

If the change leader doesn't listen then he may make a poor decision, a decision that the organization will reject. Or else the message won't be conveyed in a way that makes sense to enough people in the organization. One of our storytellers provided a good example of a change leader not communicating effectively:

> A new broom was dropped in. He thought the business was being run poorly. So he began to pull apart the business without an obvious outcome in mind. Some of what he said was true, other aspects were things we were working on. I supported some of the things he said, but the wholesale destruction of the business model was astounding. He pulled the organization apart and drove a new accountability model. We're still now in complete disarray. We know we're accountable but we don't know what we're supposed to be doing. I don't know what the purpose of the new model is, but we've seen a 30 per cent fall in efficiency, morale has dropped 40 per cent and the market's flooded with CVs. The change was done so badly, with no clear expectations established on outcomes, that it's undermined everything it was trying to achieve. I've learned you need to put that effort in up front. You can't just apply shock treatment and hope everything will be right. The change was done to us. There was no time to reflect and no dialogue. The accountability conversation was just a message – 'accountability is broken'. It's not the way we did it before. We did it slow and measured. We floated the idea past the next layer of management and the next layer and so on. It was quite a deep and measured process, then we acted on it. The work we did at the front end was gold. We asked what people thought about it, people opened up and then it was easy to frame the model. You must ask questions.

Contrast this story with some of the stories recounted in Chapter 3, in which change leaders spent time listening to their organizations before declaring what would happen next. Remember too that when change is complex, you can never be sure that your prescribed solution will work, even if you have consulted with others. Dialogue is not a one-off event that precedes effective change. Dialogue is an ongoing activity that happens across the organization all the time. The effective change leader continues to participate in the dialogue, hearing how others are making sense of ongoing events, sharing his perspective, and acting as a focal point through which a collective sense-making process can emerge.

2. *Transparency*

Forty per cent of our storytellers spoke of the importance of telling it like it is. Sometimes this was expressed in terms of transparency, sometimes in terms of being prepared to deliver the hard message, and on a couple of occasions with reference to the 'elephant in the room':

> In the end the integration was successful, but I think it could have been done better. The Japanese integration was part of a global acquisition. In Japan their brand had higher presence in their markets. When I went to their office I heard that the message being communicated was that the two organizations were merging. To motivate their employees their president told people it was a merger rather than an acquisition. The key message was 'don't worry, we'll take care of you.' So the two businesses had a different understanding of the transaction. However hard we tried there was a hidden agenda that got in the way which was that their people didn't want to be taken over by us, and we didn't think we were in the same league as them as marketers. We were an energy company first and foremost and they were a marketing organization. Nobody wanted to recognise these issues and so although measures were taken to force the two companies together, it took two years to get to the point where things were working well.

Openness and transparency came up time and again in the stories I heard. Change leaders often have to manage a desire to be open and transparent alongside a fear that openness might result in important information being leaked outside the organization. The CEO of a healthcare company decided to take the risk:

> We made the decision to begin selling through big retail. The issue was that it would take months to build up the inventory required to sell through that channel, so what did we tell staff in the meantime? If the word went out too early then we expected a backlash from the pharmacies and we would lose the chance to manage the message. In the end I decided to get the company together and tell them. I expected to get the pharmacists on the phone screaming, but it never happened. It appears the secret was kept.

A police officer in the UK told the story of a major restructure in which some senior people were going to lose their jobs:

> We needed to reduce the number of senior managers. We brought in an HR firm to help us work out how to do it. Their approach was very process driven and harsh. I thought to myself – no – I'm not going to do it that way. So we designed

a dialogue to bring the senior people together in one room to discuss what needed to be done. HR screamed – no! But it was the best thing. We were able to talk to people about their concerns, and to put something together that was humane and which was accepted because we co-generated the approach.

Contrast these stories with a story from Europe in which a public transport company attempted to become more service minded without including customers in the dialogue:

To be more service minded meant changing the rostering system. We built a full program around it including the service concept, prices, catering, uniforms and operations. It took us four months to design the program and we fitted out an old warehouse into a tangible expression of the new vision. Over the next three months we put 12,000 people through a full day induction in the warehouse. The leadership team were there at every event, shaking hands. The external world got wind of it and we weren't prepared. They summarised our intentions in terms of station closures, very negatively, right at the end of the program. Then we had to give into the unions who used the newspapers to influence customer opinions. We had to soften our plans. If we were doing it again I would bring the outside world in earlier. We were navel gazing. We created a service program without the customer being part of the program. We considered it, but felt it was too risky. We were worried about the story getting out and customers being influenced by employees in the wrong way because the employees didn't have a high opinion of management. There was a huge distance between head office and staff on the ground. We were naive.

The Director of an educational institution talked about what can happen if the organization doesn't engage in open frank dialogue:

I learned you have to tell people the truth. Don't lie and pretend and don't pretend to care if you don't, even when people don't want to hear the truth. For example, the organization wanted a new system and were told it would cost $7m. I knew it would cost $20m, but they did their best not to hear what I had to say and went ahead and commissioned it anyway. I did at least succeed in persuading them to establish an advisory committee to oversee the implementation and to keep them advised of progress. Once the advisory committee was established, there then emerged this strange game of not passing on the truth. So the committee twisted itself in knots and kept tripping up all the time. I found ways of encouraging the committee to start leaking like a sieve. People need a channel to the truth even if they don't always seem to want it.

Transparency doesn't just mean openness, it also means clarity. It may sound obvious, but the change leader needs to articulate a message that is easy for others to understand. This is harder than it sounds if the scenario is complex. The change leader may feel compelled to give people a complete understanding of the whole situation. If this serves only to confuse people, then the change leader is better off extracting the key themes of the message and constructing a simple narrative around those core themes. The next storyteller was an internal practitioner, working with the executive team of a large global multinational attempting to come up with new values for the organization:

> After several attempts to get the work going, I sent a paper to the CEO with an invitation to talk to me within the next three months. He rang me the next week and said that it was the only paper he'd read on the topic that he'd understood. You have to imagine you're talking to someone who knows absolutely nothing about the subject and use very simple, plain language to help it feel real, so that people can see how to take action. The outcome we were looking for wasn't just the words, but being able to connect the words with what was happening in the organization and to embed the meaning of the words into processes and systems. They needed time to think things through and I needed to hold the complexity. I needed to make sure the language remained simple in the face of people telling me nothing was happening and we were going too slow.

Another storyteller was responsible for transforming an organization whose existence was threatened by some of the behaviours of its leaders that resulted in heavy fines by the regulators. When I asked him what qualities he felt he had brought to the task the first quality he mentioned was

> ...bringing simplicity to complexity. So I could sit down with the CEO on a regular basis and frame where we had got to so we could get quickly to the point where I could tell him where I needed him to intervene.

Another storyteller also named being able to simplify things as the first quality he felt enabled him to be successful:

> I'm able to strategize and also to simplify things and communicate a strategy effectively so that it's understood. I challenged everyone else on the team to come up with their own elevator speeches, so that our strategies were clear, robust and understandable.

Thus the change leader is not only expected to have something to say, but to provide a perspective of events that is coherent and clear, bringing a meaning to what may initially appear an indecipherable mess (Tsoukas & Chia, 2002).

3. Authenticity

An external practitioner was asked by a CEO to help facilitate an organization-wide change programme. He arrived at the reception of a hotel where the senior executive team were meeting:

> I bumped into one of the executives at reception, checking in. We had a chat and he told me with a smile 'Everyone else can change, but I won't be'. So I told him I was leaving and headed back to my car. He came after me and we had another conversation during which he changed his tune. Never be beholden to fees and so on. I'm no good if I'm not being authentic. I have to spot the traps and avoid being seduced into belittling myself. You have to be grounded.

Most barriers to effective voicing are based on fear. Fear that others will answer back and ask me questions I can't answer, leaving me embarrassed. Fear that I may become embroiled in conflict. Fear that what I say won't be popular with important people in the organization, such that my actions end up being 'career limiting'.

Higgs and Rowland (2010) discovered that all the leaders who demonstrated the four key behaviours they identified in their aforementioned study also exhibited high levels of self-awareness. You can train leaders to structure effective stories but can you really tell a good story about your relationship with change without having a good idea what your relationship to change really is? One of our storytellers told us a tale about an experience of change in which they found it difficult at times to voice the business agenda authentically:

> In the 80s and 90s there were cost pressures and some pretty brutal tactics were used to try and implement savings. I took up a job to manage a heavily unionised workforce that was all riled up. I got to be their boss, and had to reduce staff numbers as one of several cost reduction measures. I asked myself if what I was implementing was right. We were further cutting the numbers when other parts of the business weren't worrying about a million dollars here or there. We did what we had to do in order to comply with what we were instructed by the business, but I saw fallacy in it. It seemed apparent we could have sought and found more staff efficiencies and business opportunities before reducing staff numbers.

Effective voicing is authentic, and authenticity is not a skill. Authenticity emerged so strongly from the research that the whole of Chapter 10 is dedicated to it.

Storytelling

A lot of books have been written about storytelling. Sixteen per cent of our storytellers mentioned storytelling explicitly, emphasizing the value of constructing a coherent narrative. Some texts on storytelling focus on the structure of the story. Structure is important; all good stories share a similar underlying structure, but the aspects of storytelling that emerged from our research were resonance, transparency and authenticity.

The resulting story is likely to be powerful and compelling. The CEO of a media organization spoke about his success in transforming an organization that had been losing more than $150m a year. The organization had got used to failure:

> It was like Munchausen's syndrome, like when a mother wants her child to be ill so she can keep nursing it. The business was like that. We had to turn it round quickly. That meant reviewing the product, the brand and the service infrastructure. You need true grit, staying true to what you know needs to be done and keep doing it. The key is having a clear narrative. We live by narratives. You must know and believe in a genuine narrative. If you don't know your destination then you'll run out of provisions and get lost. That narrative needs to be constantly revisited and refreshed.

Note the word 'refreshed'. Having a great story to tell is not about telling it once and sticking to it. The effective change leader is engaged in an ongoing dialogue and is continually reflecting on other's responses to the narrative. As circumstances change, so does the way in which people make meaning of the organization and its environment, and so the effective narrative must also change.

KEY POINTS

- People look to others to help them make sense of the events around them.

- The members of an organization look to its leadership to provide a possible interpretation of those events, hoping that the message will reflect their own view of the world, will be open and transparent, and that it will be delivered by someone whose word can be relied upon.

- Effective change leaders express themselves based on a good understanding of other's ambitions, hopes and concerns.

- Effective change leaders are committed to be as honest and open as they possibly can be. Within any organization there will be people advising the cautious approach. It often pays to be bold, taking the opportunity to demonstrate trust in people.

- To say what feels right and true to the individual requires self-awareness and authenticity.

Reflection

05

To my surprise, many of those people kind enough to spend an hour or more of their busy lives telling me stories thanked me for it. For some people, having the space and time to talk to someone in confidence about an important event in their working lives creates new meaning. Listening to the stories, at times it felt like I was privy to the inner workings of the story-teller's mind.

Reflection as abstraction

Stacey (2012) defines reflection as abstraction – extracting oneself from the day-to-day and considering our experiences from afar. For Stacey 'all forms of thinking about and reflecting upon experience necessarily involve abstracting or drawing away from that experience'. For someone who reflects, therefore, life consists of drawing in and pulling away, being in the moment and standing back from the moment. Tsoukas (2009) makes a similar point, talking about our ongoing attachment to everyday reality, a reality that blinkers us, limiting our awareness of what else is happening around us. To appreciate the complexity of a situation, we have to stand back from the day-to-day and reflect on the greater whole.

In the introduction to *Leadership Without Easy Answers*, Heifetz (1994) talks about the complexity of modern-day life and the propensity of people generally to look for simple solutions, solutions that are often ineffective. He goes on to identify five principles of adaptive leadership, a very different frame to traditional texts. Leadership, Heifetz says, is both active and reflective, and the leader must alternate between participating and observing. He talks about how easy it is to get sucked in to participating, or doing, and suggests a list of questions that help the leader get into a space where he can see the key patterns. A list of questions sounds great but what many people find difficult, in my experience, is making time to read the list.

Sucked in

People seem busier these days. The people I coach today seem busier than the people I coached five years ago. Technology presents challenges as well as opportunities. Whereas people may once have chosen to reflect during their journey to work, or at home with a glass of wine, or even in the middle of a boring meeting or workshop, now we have mobile devices that allow us to be on-the-job 24 hours a day.

Last year one of my coachees expressed concerns that he ran from meeting to meeting. This wasn't how he wanted to be perceived, he said, as someone constantly in a hurry with no time to spare. He worked up to 70 hours a week and was still struggling to pack everything in. As we talked it became apparent that he wanted to respond to everyone who asked for his help. Initially he took small steps in the right direction, declining meeting requests and managing his diary more discriminately. This wasn't easy and he reported feeling deeply disappointed when others remarked that his availability 'sucked'. He identified a perfectionist tendency within, a desire not to let anything fall over or let other people down. In about our third session, as we discussed the bigger picture including his key work goals and career goals, he sighed and pointed at the empty coffee mug that stood on the table between us. 'Right at this moment, I'm here,' he said, pointing at the edge of the cup, 'but most of the time I'm in there,' and he pointed at the dregs at the bottom of the cup. He built a plan based on the metaphor, determining to be purposeful as to where on the mug he was standing at any one time. A few weeks later I saw him again and he was excited. He told a story about having been faced by an apparently intractable problem. Instead of becoming frustrated by the lack of progress, he explained, he chose to step up to the rim of the mug. Once there he saw two or three options he hadn't seen before. One of those options proved to be effective in solving the issue in a somewhat novel way.

More and more people want to talk about prioritization, which usually ends up as a conversation about how to make more time to reflect on why I'm doing what I'm doing. How to spend less time doing and more time reflecting on why I'm doing what I'm doing and what I could be doing differently.

The expectations of others may not help. Within many organizations there is a prevailing culture that values 'doing' over 'thinking' to the extent that there never seems time to think or reflect. People start the day with a list of things to do, and assess their productivity based on the number of boxes they managed to tick by the time they go home. The flow of messages into people's e-mails is steady, fast and unrelenting. Life becomes a constant juggling exercise in which to stop and think is to step back and watch the balls all crash to the floor.

A senior manager reporting into the CEO spoke about how he made sure he didn't get sucked into too much detail:

> I asked a colleague to agree to providing me with real-time feedback. Everyone was head down and focused on today and I needed to be scanning the horizon. I asked myself on a regular basis, 'How's our ecosystem doing?' I continually assessed my world, the roles, the ecosystem out to the community and watched to see how all the moving parts worked together; connecting the dots and understanding the intricacies of relationships.

Sometimes even the most senior executive teams don't spend enough time reflecting, sucked in to the everyday pressure to get things done. This internal practitioner's role was to help the senior executive team of a global multi-national agree on the organization's values. At first the executive saw it as their responsibility to define those values on behalf of everyone else. They were surprised to find their efforts rejected:

> At first some of them went straight to 'I know the answer.' But you need real meaning and a huge bunch of people getting it. The senior team didn't like that and so they rolled out their values to a group of a few hundred senior managers. People said things like, 'Whatever…' and, 'Why didn't you have the respect to ask me?' and, 'This is a ridiculous waste of time.' I told the executive that the process is important, that it needed to be messy before it became clear. For the words to matter we needed to explore the dissonance between how they acted and the words, and to explore what they might need to do to shift things. That meeting with the senior managers became the catalyst for a period of deep reflection lasting three to four months.

Reflection in practice

Fourteen per cent of the storytellers specifically spoke about reflection. For example, a CEO spoke about the role of the leader:

> It's my role to engage people in dialogue. To sit with a group and ask, for example, why they're here in the first place. You need to create the time to talk to people, to think and reflect.

Another leader talked about creating space for his team to reflect:

> With the leadership team I made sure we spent time reflecting together at every meeting. What's happening? What's the current conversation? We discussed and collectively responded. We developed strategy on the run, recognizing hot spots and how to address them.

If reflection is about abstraction, or simply giving serious thought to something, then reflection can take many forms, including:

- Going away for a week to contemplate in silence the world and my place in it.
- Taking time at the end of the day or week to think about what's just happened.
- Taking a couple of minutes after a specific event to think about the impact of my behaviours.
- Taking a second or two during an event to consider what I am about to say next.
- Sitting down with others to think together and engage in dialogue.

As with listening, it may not be useful to talk about whether people reflect or not; most people would say that they spend at least some of their time standing back and thinking about the consequences of their actions. At issue may be the amount of time people spend reflecting and the nature of that reflection.

Reflecting on external events

Twenty-six per cent of our storytellers spoke directly of the importance of abstraction; standing back and viewing their businesses from afar. For example, the CEO of a failing retail business in Spain said:

> Competition was getting tougher and the economy was getting weaker. It was clear we needed to radically rethink the organizational model, look at the cost base and centralize some functions. We need to move from a company-operated model to a franchise model, which was radical for Spain. We needed to automate the supply chain, reduce staff and find an upside in synergies and think nationally.

The incoming CEO of a not-for-profit organization spoke of the need to restructure his business:

> One of the reasons I was successful was that I had that outside experience; I understood the external environment. I had an insight into the challenges

and changes taking place in the sector, and could see we had no solid core; no investment in business services, HR, no demand for excellence, no KPIs and no accountability. Clients were becoming more difficult and we needed to structure differently to meet their needs.

The CEO of a not-for-profit talked about an ongoing process of continuous thinking:

> As a new CEO I needed to think about how to drive change. We needed a constant which for us was around values and the mission of the organization. I had to reframe the mission. How did I determine it? I asked myself questions – how can we deliver on why we exist? I recognized that the entire system needed to work effectively. We were part of a system, but playing a small part and leaving the rest of the system to their own devices. We weren't impacting, but being impacted. External trends were happening and we weren't responding. I needed a picture of how everything fitted together to achieve the mission. The process continues now because change is constant.

Most of us expect our leaders to stand back and think about the external environment in this way. But reflection isn't only about considering what's happening in the outside world.

Reflecting on self

In a classic article called 'Teaching smart people how to learn', Argyris (1991) differentiated between single-loop and double-loop learning. Single-loop learners rely on their logical/rational capability; their intellectual mastery. A problem is rigorously analysed and the logical solution deduced. If a solution fails, then the single-loop learner is most likely to attribute the cause of that failure to an unexpected external event or someone else's behaviour. The double-loop learner, on the other hand, sees herself as a variable and is more likely to question her own role in events. The double-loop learner is therefore interested in self, and in becoming more self-aware.

If dialogue sits at the heart of change then the change leader has an ongoing role to play in guiding change through engaging in dialogue. In Chapter 3 I framed the importance of listening without an agenda, being able to immerse oneself in another person's meaning, seeking to understand the origin of that meaning in terms of other people's values and beliefs. This is hard to do in practice. Often we find ourselves triggered to respond in the moment, compelled to defend a point of view or to correct an assumption that to us seems false. At this point we revert to our own agendas, and become focused on voicing. Dialogue becomes monologue and the conversation reverts to becoming an exchange of views. The trigger is almost always a thought in the moment, which in turn leads to an emotion, which in turn leads to a decision to assert a particular point of view. All of this happens in the moment and is hard to manage.

The single-loop learner may not acknowledge her role in any breakdown in dialogue. She is more likely to attribute responsibility to the person voicing the comment that evoked the emotion. The double-loop learner owns her role in the process and seeks to understand how she is most often triggered so that she can become familiar with and better manage the process in the moment.

This is not to say that the self-reflection process is solely about the origin of one's emotions. In the context of leadership authenticity, Avolio and Gardner (2005) cite four particular aspects of self-awareness, all of which emerged in our research: purpose, identity, values and emotions. Purpose (Chapters 4 and 10), identity (Chapter 8) and values (Chapter 10) are covered elsewhere in this book, and may all form the basis for reflection. Emotions are the 'pointy end' of values, identity and purpose. We may feel angry if our values are offended, anxious if our identity is threatened and frustrated if others don't appear to align with our preferred purpose. The process by which our individual emotions are triggered has a lot to tell us about who we are, what we believe in and the assumptions we make.

Twenty-eight per cent of our storytellers spoke about managing emotions. For example, a CEO talked about walking into a sales conference where he was due to deliver an engaging speech:

> One time I went to a sales conference where there were 300 people and I didn't want to be there. It was my job to rev them up, but I didn't feel like it. I had just received some bad news and it showed. I received feedback afterwards that said I looked distracted and didn't answer questions well. You have to leave the bad news at the door otherwise it creates a lot of stress. You have to internalize a lot and not always wear your heart on your sleeve. You've got to be yourself and be respectful to the role. Good leaders leave the last conversation at the door.

Another storyteller talked about failing to manage the way he felt about a particular individual over a prolonged period of time:

> One area I could have done better was in dealing with X, Y's right-hand man. I thought he was a duplicitous snake but what I did was wrong. I showed my disdain and disrespect in the way I worked with him. I should have got to understand him and use that to my advantage, but I didn't like him and it showed.

One of our storytellers spoke about being aware of his emotions and the need to manage and reflect upon them on a regular basis:

> People want to go into task and transaction mode but you can't get away from the human element. You're dealing with emotions 24 hours, seven days a week. Yours and other's. There's no magic book on dealing with humans and human emotions. You have to accept your feelings and go through the emotional gamut every day. Today I met with three people; three sets of emotions and me as the leader having to be neutral, helping them through it. I try and stay earthed, plugged in to what I believe in.

The effective change leader therefore spends time reflecting on her own role in events, including the link between her values and beliefs, her emotions and the behaviours she exhibits. By reflecting regularly on her emotions the change leader not only becomes progressively more self-aware, but also more attuned to similar processes being experienced by others.

Managing other's emotions

Developing a better understanding of our emotions helps us understand better the emotions of others. We need to pay attention to emotion and to reflect on people's emotional responses to change if we are to navigate successfully through complexity. Smollan and Sayers (2009) talk about the strong emotional undertones underlying all organizational cultures and argue that the consequences of damaging that emotional fabric can be severe. Change leaders who attempt to implement change from afar without attending to these emotional undertones will have little insight into this process.

An internal practitioner spoke about the need to cultivate management's capacity to manage emotions. She spoke about a major change that took place in a European business with lots of country subsidiaries:

> Change has an impact on people, including job losses. We need to provide support which includes being there on site. We need to help them deal with the pushback and make sure they empower their first line managers, who will be most exposed to the emotional pushback. We hold local workshops specifically for those frontline managers and talk to them about dealing with emotions.

Sometimes the change leader may need to focus up more than down:

> The board was fearful of ceding power to grocery, but people wanted to shop in grocery and if we weren't there they would buy second- and third-tier brands. The question was, would we sell through this particular retailer? I went to see

the CEO of the retail organization and co-opted him into selling the idea to our board; I got him to present to them. I spent time with ex-buyers and got to understand how we would have to change our thinking and processes and gave the board the assurances they needed. In the end I got the go ahead.

The need to engage with the entire organization emotionally was identified by several of our storytellers. For example, the president of a European energy business spoke of the importance of being able to make a strong logical case for a change programme that included significant redundancies, but also of the need to engage with the emotional side of change:

There was a big emotional piece to manage. Seeing 25 per cent of your colleagues leaving, entering a tough job market, is hard. The only way to address it was through open and honest dialogue, making sure open conversations were happening at all levels. Many of my leadership team had been in the business a long time and knew people up and down the hierarchy, so it was easier to understand what was going on behind the scenes. Through the networks it was easy to see the signals and recognize the emotional connection. The emotional connection is about understanding what's going on, the bit that numbers don't tell you. For us it was easy because we knew the people. It's tough if you don't know the people; to know what's happening.

Many writers have pointed out the role of emotions in behaviour, and suggested that effective leaders are able to better manage their emotions in the moment, and recognize and respond effectively to the emotions of others. To attend to the emotions of others requires spending time reflecting on the origins of those emotions and how best to engage accordingly.

KEY POINTS

- To reflect is to abstract oneself from the immediacy of events. Many of us get so sucked into doing that we don't spend enough time reflecting.

- There are lots of different ways to reflect, by oneself and with others.

- Reflecting on events and the behaviours of others is one focus for reflection.

- To participate effectively in dialogue it helps to develop an enhanced understanding of our emotional responses.

- Tuning into the origins of our emotions helps us to tune into the emotions of others.

PART TWO
Perspective, purpose and identity

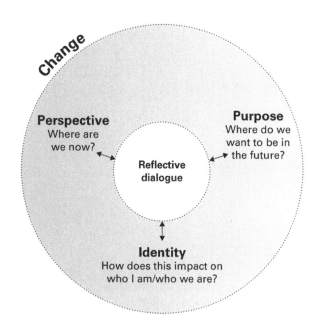

The evolution of perspective

06

In this part of the book we turn to both the context for, and outcomes of, reflective dialogue in action. In this chapter we discuss the evolution of shared perspectives. We rarely enter into interactions with others without a perspective. We take pre-existing perspectives into interactions with us. If the interaction is monologic then we are likely to leave the interaction with the same perspective we came in with. If the interaction is dialogic then we are likely to depart the interaction with a different point of view, newly informed by the perspective of the other person.

Fifty-six per cent of our storytellers talked about the importance of gathering multiple perspectives, the fourth most mentioned factor by the storytellers. The emerging change model links the quality of dialogue with the evolution of shared perspective. Perspectives form both an input to dialogue and an outcome from dialogue, as perspectives continue to shift and change over the course of time. When dialogue stops, the collective perspective fragments.

The paradoxical theory of change

The more people share a common view of the way things are today, the more likely they are to come together around a common intention for the future. Beisser (1970) expressed this eloquently more than 40 years ago in outlining his paradoxical theory of change:

> Briefly stated, it is this: that change occurs when one becomes what he is, not when he tries to become what he is not. Change does not take place through a coercive attempt by the individual or by another person to change him, but it does take place if one takes the time and effort to be what he is – to be fully invested in his current positions.

One of our storytellers articulated a similar philosophy in describing where he first started in attempting to align his new team around a future vision. He had joined the company recently as the CEO. The company had been losing money for several years and had become the problem child of the larger parent company. If it continued to fail it was likely to be sold off or broken up:

> For the team the key moment was when I said we were going to have an offsite. The team complained, saying that previous offsites had achieved little in terms of agreeing a future direction. I told them we weren't going to talk about the future, we were going to talk about the present; the state of the market, the competition, what we were all doing. They were surprised by what they learnt and the silos started to break down. Without that insight across the business they wouldn't have understood what I eventually took to the board.

This implies that the emergence of a compelling vision is usually preceded by a gathering of perspectives on the present. Not all change initiatives start with this focus on the present; often the dialogue is directed straight away to future vision.

While it may be true to say that to engage people around a vision we ought first to encourage the expression of perspectives on the present, the ECM is not really sequential. Perspectives and visions are forever shifting and changing, and if perspectives on the present are always changing, so are people's visions of a future state. By ensuring the organization engages in dialogue, the change leader is effectively ensuring that perspectives on the present and future remain broadly aligned.

The effective change leader's commitment to reflective dialogue makes it more likely that the organization as a whole will share a coherent perspective on the present. The change leader who listens enhances his own understanding of what is happening, role-models the same behaviour in others, thereby encouraging others to share and test their understandings. The change leader who voices, provides others with a perspective to 'try on for size' in their quest to make sense of what's happening. The change leader who reflects continually reviews where people have got to on the journey and what they need in order to be able to carry on making sense of the organization and its environment. Without dialogue it is unlikely that the organization will come to share a common perspective on the present, let alone the future.

The significance of multiple perspectives

The story of the elephant and the blind men illustrates the significance of multiple perspectives well. In one version of the story six blind men were asked to determine what an elephant looked like by feeling different parts of the elephant's body. The blind man who felt a leg said the elephant was like a pillar; the one who felt the tail said the elephant was like a rope; the one who felt the trunk said the elephant was like a tree branch; the one who felt the ear said the elephant was like a hand fan; the one who felt the belly said the elephant was like a wall; and the one who felt the tusk said the elephant was like a solid pipe. The blind men heard what each other had to say and argued in front of the king as to who was right. The king then explained to them 'All of you are right. The reason every one of you is telling it differently is because each one of you touched the different part of the elephant. So, actually the elephant has all the features you mentioned.'

People's perspectives shift and change. Boje (2012) tells the story of a play called 'Tamara', performed in Los Angeles on multiple stages. In the play 12 characters tell their stories before an audience that is invited to follow the characters around the set, choosing which characters to follow as they move independently from stage to stage. The audience is faced with ongoing choices as to which character to follow from scene to scene through different scenarios. By the end of the play each member of the audience has experienced a different story. Because there are so many different possible journeys, even a group of six or seven people comparing experiences after the play won't have a complete collective view as to what happened. Each person leaves with a different sense of what's happened, a different emotional attachment to different characters and a different sense of justice and injustice, perspectives that shifted and changed from scene to scene.

This is a wonderful metaphor for what happens in any complex changing environment: different people experiencing different events at different times, enjoying different perspectives that continue to shape and evolve. No single perspective at any one time represents the whole. As we've seen, many leaders at the top of an organization manage this challenge by seeking data, but the data, even if available, are unlikely to tell the whole story. In the meantime groups of people meet within the organization, often informally and/or virtually, to compare stories and come up with their own collective views as to what constitutes the 'truth'.

Without a 'dialogic' process it is likely that the organization will coalesce into a network of coalitions (Rodgers, 2007) of which the senior leadership team may be just one. These different coalitions often appear to compete with each other, seeking to privilege their own perspective as 'truth' and the change agenda gets stuck.

Failing to recognize the significance of multiple perspectives

One of our storytellers was the human resources director of a large multinational that made a series of significant acquisitions over a short time. After a period of intense activity the new organization settled down to run the new business. The senior executives set about their task with enthusiasm, spreading the message that the organization was now one company with one set of goals and objectives and one way of doing things. The company subsequently went through some tough times, partly because different people, coming from different heritage organizations, had difficulty in understanding each other. Each heritage organization had its own way of doing things reflected in its own use of language: people used the same language to mean different things. These were difficult years in which the company suffered a number of highly publicized setbacks.

What, our storyteller wondered, could the company have done differently? One aspect of the story stood out for him – the day shortly after the last acquisition when the senior executive team declared that the new company was now one company with a single new identity such that there was no need to spend any more time discovering how different people viewed the world post-merger and acquisition. While well intended, this declaration effectively blinded the executive team to the reality, which was that the new organization *wasn't* a single entity and that different people had different perspectives on what had happened, what was happening, and what constituted a desirable future. Our storyteller reflected:

> People's heritage can't be brushed aside. After a big merger or acquisition you can't just say, 'We're all one company now and that's it.' Even today, ten years later, there are people in one of the companies we acquired who have been watching who's done well and who's not done so well. They look at the top team now and see lots of their old bosses in that team and say that they've won!

For the change leader, facilitating a common perspective may be harder than it sounds, for when we are already invested in a particular perspective we tend to listen from our agenda. It is difficult for most of us to listen from a different agenda. We may jump quickly to conclusions as to the validity of that agenda or the motivations of the person espousing it. We may find ourselves labelling the other person as 'resistant to change', which usually means 'resistant to my agenda'. The other person may experience me as equally 'resistant'.

Sharing perspectives

Several of our storytellers described processes they used to facilitate the sharing of multiple perspectives. Internal and external practitioners are often deployed for this; people expert in working with large groups, capable of managing some of the tensions that often arise from such gatherings who may be regarded as being to some degree external to the process. We heard a few such stories in which a practitioner team convened a large group of people to work through a predetermined process designed to help people understand each other's perspectives. We also came across a couple of more unusual processes. This storyteller was a CEO, brought in to transform a not-for-profit organization:

> We set up a consultative committee of our own accord. It represented a
> cross-section of geography, function and seniority. A person could be on the
> committee for two years, and the role of the committee was to raise issues with
> us and be there for us to consult with them on specific issues and participate in
> building solutions. It was really good stuff and helped us in the overall change.
> When we did something we could come back, report on what we'd done and
> ask them for feedback.

The key message from the stories, however, was that it's not the method that matters as much as the willingness and capability of the change leader to create a safe space for people to engage in dialogue. In most organizations the importance of consultation is recognized, and some simple practices established to achieve it, the most common of which is the team meeting. The problem with focusing too much on method is that the importance of a commitment to dialogue may be overlooked. So it is that we see managers at many meetings switch off completely from what is happening around them and spend much of their time working through their e-mails on a mobile device. People are meeting, but they are not connecting.

Perspectives and purpose

Without some degree of shared perspective as to what is going on in the present, it is highly unlikely that an organization will succeed in rallying round a common purpose. This means that if the change leader wants to rally the organization around a new future, the place to start is with the here and now. In siloed organizations this is no easy task. In an organization that is perceived to be failing, the sales people may blame the IT people for not providing the systems required to deliver data on time. The marketing people may blame the sales people for offering big discounts contrary to the desired brand proposition. The finance people may blame the logistics people for holding excessive inventory. The product development people may blame the technical people for being unable to develop the new products on time. The COO may blame the product development people for designing the wrong product and the CEO may blame the COO for focusing on product development and not IT. If we then add geography as another layer, the problem is compounded, with the UK business blaming the French business, the China business blaming the Korean business and so on. In these scenarios most people are invested in their own perspective, their own sense of what's right and wrong and what needs to be changed. Until those people are able to put aside their convictions for a while and authentically explore the perspectives of others, the organization has little chance of achieving a shared understanding of the multiplicity of issues currently facing it, let alone deciding upon a new future.

In Chapter 7 we'll continue this discussion, shifting our attention to the emergence of common purpose.

KEY POINTS

- In any complex scenario no single person or team has access to the whole story.

- Everyone has an individual perspective, and some teams may have collective perspectives that seem real and 'true'. Attachment to the 'truth' of one's own perspective acts as a barrier to dialogue.

- The best place to start in building vision is by spending time on the here-and-now.

- By committing to dialogue people are committing to the possibility that their perspective of the here-and-now is open to change.

The evolution of purpose

07

Sharing a common purpose or vision for the future was mentioned by 68 per cent of our storytellers. Early on in the storytelling process I was struck by an apparent paradox. Contrast these two stories. The first story comes from an oil production company. The company was being run by a multinational oil company through a joint venture partnership with the national government:

> Targets weren't being met and hadn't been for several years. The JV partners were demanding better performance, but it wasn't happening, and all we had was an ongoing feud. No one in the company thought that performance was about to improve and so they were just getting used to being bashed. The company hired a new CEO who quickly recognized that the old strategy wasn't going to deliver. He didn't have a clear idea as to what the new strategy needed to be and said that the first thing we needed to do was to come up with a new and common view of the future, one that would reenergize the company, because without that energy it was obvious we weren't going to deliver. The task was to come up with an idea, a powerful vision. People had dabbled in the past, but they were used to top management telling what the vision was going to be. The CEO and the top team decided to engage the organization in co-creating something. I designed and led a two-day workshop for 400 people, the objective of which was to craft a new vision. People shared perspectives on what was facing them and built a business case for the new future. We set a five-year vision and worked backwards to create goals one, two, three and four years out.

The second story comes from a private equity partner whose firm bought out a retailer from its parent company. He became the CEO of the company once it became independent:

> I went in with a clear idea of what we needed to do. We had a 90-day plan, a six-month plan, a one-year plan, etc. Two of us led the development of the investment thesis and set about executing the pre-formed plan. We executed it and sold the business for nine times our investment in less than four years. It was a pretty simple thesis; we gave an unloved division of a big corporate some love.

In the first story the future of the company is co-created by the employees of that company. In the second story it sounds as if the vision was effectively imposed. We might place the two stories at either end of a spectrum such as that described by Senge *et al* (1994), which suggests there are five starting points in building a shared vision. At one end of the spectrum is 'telling', in which the senior management of a firm tell people what the vision is and then ask them to get excited about it. At the other end of the spectrum is 'co-creating', in which the vision is built together. Senge *et al* suggest that 'telling' represents a more authoritative approach, and they predict that organizations will increasingly embrace 'co-creation' as being more engaging and participative.

The stories we heard don't appear to support this model. The first storyteller describes an inclusive process that was only partially successful because some members of the organization ultimately didn't commit. The second storyteller describes an organization where it sounds like the vision was imposed, yet people seem highly engaged and productive. So what's going on?

All visions are co-created

The Senge *et al* (1994) model appears to imply that some organizational visions are co-created while others are imposed. This is because the model focuses purely on the organization. From a different perspective, where we can see not only the organization, but the industry, the world and everyone in it, we can see that for all intents and purposes *all* visions are co-created. The purely organizational perspective appears to reinforce the 'great man' frame of leadership in which one person comes up with a vision and then seeks to impose it on others. While there are people out there who may identify with this version of leadership, is this really what happens?

Charles Darwin is accredited by many as having come up with the theory of evolution based on natural selection. In fact Darwin was heavily influenced by the work of Thomas Robert Malthus. Furthermore, shortly before publishing *On the Origin of Species*, Darwin was dismayed to discover that Alfred Russel Wallace had developed a very similar theory, such that the two of them presented their theories together to the Linnaean Society. This perspective doesn't lend itself well to our collective western belief in the greatness of the individual, and so the story is usually told somewhat differently. Darwin gets the credit and the theory of evolution is 'Darwinian'.

Similarly, Francis Crick and James Watson were the first to come up with the molecular model of DNA. This was of course a remarkable achievement, but it wasn't achieved in isolation. Much of the data they had access to were collected by researchers in other laboratories. Crick and Watson specifically acknowledged the work of Maurice Wilkins, Rosalind Franklin and others at King's College London. Indeed Watson later wrote that he had access to some of Franklin's data without her having known. The molecular model of DNA might more accurately be said to have emerged from the interactions between different groups of researchers working in different laboratories, but it was Crick and Watson who got to press first, and they who got most of the credit.

None of this is to devalue the contribution that any of these people made to their fields of science. The popular discourse, however, is overly individualistic. Darwin was contemplating the origins of mankind at a particular time and place; a time and place it was considered appropriate and safe to pursue such thoughts, and at a time when society was prepared to invest in sending people around the world to study such things. If it hadn't been Darwin, it would have been Wallace, and if it hadn't been Wallace, it would have been someone else. Darwin was in effect the focal point at which multiple insights converged into the one beautifully expressed holistic insight. Similarly, it was arguably Francis Crick who had both the data and the experience working with x-ray diffraction data for other large molecules with helical symmetry, who had the first eureka moment. But if hadn't been Crick it would have been Wilkins or Franklin, or one of the researchers at one of the other laboratories. Crick and Watson became the locus at which a *collective* insight was most eloquently expressed. Our culture abounds with such stories, all of them individualistic: Newton sitting under a tree full of ripe apples, Archimedes in his bath. The point is that before Archimedes got into his bath he had been interacting with others.

So the CEO who arrives with a ready-made vision didn't come up with that vision in isolation. The vision is a consequence of his interactions with others outside the organization if not inside. The vision is no less co-created than a vision formed in collaboration with the members of the organization; it's just co-created with *other* people.

With this frame in mind, let's play the tape a little longer on the 'great man' story recounted above:

> Yes, it was a simple thesis, a textbook approach I had seen used before by others at the companies where I had worked. I hoped it was directionally correct, but had I got it wrong, well then I would have copped it on the chin and said so.

So just because the CEO had a vision for the future didn't mean he wasn't open to it continuing to evolve. This next storyteller also went into the organization with a largely formed vision, but did some work on it first with other stakeholders:

> I felt I needed a story to attract the right people. I had an idea of the vision – to be the leading pre-eminent company in our field, but I tested it with some key stakeholders and they laughed. They were much more focused on cost than on creating value, so I changed it to one of the leading companies in our field. Being the leader wouldn't have been considered credible.

This story comes from the CEO of another not-for-profit:

> The organization had an existing mission but it was only moderately successful. As the new CEO I had to think about how to drive change and I needed a constant. That constant had to be the mission of the company and its values. It was clear that different stakeholders had different motivations. I couldn't throw out the existing mission and supplant it with a new one; I needed to recast the mission. Some of the words needed to be recast and the definition of some of the words reviewed. Once we redefined the words, then people wanted it, because it was consistent with what they already believed in. The process is continuing now and is constantly changing.

These stories, in which new CEOs joined companies with a pretty good idea of the direction they wanted to take, are not stories of visions being imposed on organizations. In each case there is a strong sense of the leader being open to the further evolution of that vision through ongoing dialogue. If that commitment to dialogue is absent then things may go wrong. One of our storytellers accepted a new role as the HR director of a big financial company:

> When I went into the job I wanted to change the way the company did HR. My perspective was based on the four-level of model of HR where the first level is administration and level four is strategist. I wanted to take it to level two, perhaps three, and I didn't think the HR team I inherited had the right capabilities. I thought they couldn't see what they couldn't deliver, they couldn't write the plan, so I brought in an HR guru from the US and I wrote an extensive paper on what I planned to do by myself. I didn't bring people along with me though and people didn't see things the way I saw them. I replaced seven of the top nine people in 12 months and the people below freaked out and decided they weren't going to play. HR people saw things from the perspective of their businesses, not as members of an HR community. I thought I could do it over night, but I couldn't.

This is a different kind of story. In the first three stories the new CEOs came with a vision of what needed to happen, but also appeared committed to constructive dialogue and to seeking out multiple perspectives. Embedded in their narratives is a recognition that the change narrative is not a constant, but is something that shifts and changes as a consequence of changes in the environment and the dialogue that takes place around those changes.

Visions are dynamic

Consider the following story from the CEO of an equity partnership charged with managing the construction of a major property development in China.

> I had public shareholders to look after outside of China. The company listed at $3 but then the real estate market collapsed as did access to equity. It became about trying to keep our nose above water. We couldn't turn off the development plans because it was a big project for China, a major event. They'd already built a new highway, a rail-line, an airport, etc. The value of the company fell to 5 cents, but the Chinese weren't too concerned. They would default on their loans, but the banks couldn't do anything about it. The project simply went on hold. The Chinese were OK with that – they were in it for the long haul. My offshore shareholders were very concerned though. At that point the goalposts changed, and the focus became avoiding bankruptcy. Bankruptcy would have been considered a failure. I worked really hard and eventually managed to refinance the company. My overseas shareholders respected what I'd done in a very challenging situation and recommended me to be considered to run a new turnaround opportunity.

In this extreme case, about a tough assignment in a foreign market at about the time of the GFC, the shareholder's aspirations for the equity partnership shifted from building a highly profitable new property to the avoidance of bankruptcy. This didn't happen without a great deal of angst and tension, but the CEO succeeded in uniting one group of stakeholders around a new vision.

The environment changes, people's perspectives of that environment change, as does the view of where the company needs to be. The process through which the vision evolves and a new collective vision emerges is dialogue. Without dialogue it is likely that opinions as to the causes of change will fragment. People with different views will compete with each other to tell the most convincing story and the organization will find itself divided as to the best way forward.

The acting CEO of a not-for-profit organization talked about why she felt her company had got stuck:

> The problem was the purpose, and still is, I think. Within the organization we have a general level of agreement, the core members anyway. In the office I'd say two-thirds are on board, some don't care and a few are resisters. The problem is the board. They're split as to what the organization exists to do.

The role of the change leader

Visioning is thus a social process, but as we discussed in Chapter 5, the change leader is expected to have a view of where the organization is headed. For this reason some of our storytellers wanted to go into their new organizations with some kind of story to tell. But the successful storytellers didn't seek to defend that vision to the death: they all spoke of being open to the possibility of change, indeed an expectation that eventually new circumstances would require a new way forward. In this sense our change leaders are like Darwin, Watson and Crick. By engaging in dialogue not only within their organizations but also outside of their organizations, they become the lightning rod to which all perspectives are drawn, and from which emerge visions that are in essence co-created.

Many of our storytellers openly acknowledged this role. This storyteller, for example, talked about a major restructure within an energy company: 'You have to anchor everything to a clear outcome that everyone can see. People need to be able to look at it and say, "Yeah, I see that".' An external practitioner spoke more broadly about how important it is for the organization to know where it wants to go:

> Change fails when organizations don't know what they want. There's not enough work done upfront to agree what the right thing is to do. Where there's a coherent story and a road map to enable people to see what's coming, that's when it works well. This is what it means for us as a story, rather than people being bombarded with lots of separate communications. People want to know what it means to them. What will be different?

Who to engage in the visioning?

One of our storytellers told the story of his being appointed to a role in Russia, working for a joint venture company that sought foreign customers to sign up to long-term contracts for its natural resources. The company had been talking to customers in China and Korea for several years already, but nothing had been agreed. A feasibility study was required, but there was no consensus as to how they should go about doing it and no one was driving it forward. Our storyteller succeeded in engaging effectively with the Chinese, the Koreans and the local Russian organization. Feasibility studies were conducted and documented and all the signs were good. However, when it came to getting final approvals for the documents the project fell over. One of the main reasons was that one of the national state companies stepped in, pulled apart the feasibility study and declared the need to conduct their own marketing study. Progress slowed and the project was shelved. Our storyteller explained:

> It was the one thing we didn't do. I don't think they believed we would succeed in getting the feasibility study signed, and when we did they thought we'd pulled a fast one. They inserted themselves, pulled apart the study and decided they wanted sole rights. We didn't engage them early enough. I'm not Russian and not part of the circle, and the Russian members of the team recognized that only belatedly. We, and the other shareholders, didn't embrace the greater Russian state early enough.

When and how to engage the internal organization? The message from our storytellers is that the internal organization must be engaged, through dialogue, but that doesn't mean the organization will always be able to come up with an adequate vision by itself. Especially if an organization has been run along autocratic, hierarchical lines for a long time, it may prove hard to engage in dialogue about the future. The people who really cared may have already departed. This is not to commend some kind of diagnostic by which to decide whether or not it is appropriate to engage an organization in dialogue. The message from the storytellers is *engage, engage, engage*, but the change leader shouldn't necessarily expect that the collective internal perspective will always be sufficient to come up with a vision that feels intuitively right.

External perspectives

Fourteen per cent of our storytellers spoke explicitly about the importance of seeking out external perspectives. In Chapter 3 we included the story of the CEO of a global energy business who chose to visit the competition before visiting his own organization. Spending time with the competition helped him work out what questions to ask.

Not seeking out the external perspective can lead to disappointing outcomes. In Chapter 4 we told the story of the customer service initiative that floundered, partly because the organization didn't include its customers in the process. In this chapter you have just read the Russian story in which the storyteller regretted that key external stakeholders weren't engaged earlier.

A senior leader spoke about the experience of his CEO. They worked for a print media organization in which the owners didn't appear to seek the perspectives of the outside world, or indeed the views of most people working inside the organization:

> In that organization the editor is God; all seeing, all knowing, all wise. They are seen as a barometer, the beating pulse of the nation, but it's all bullshit. They're all in their late 40s and 50s, all men, all Caucasian, with Anglo-Celtic names, who in the main eschew analysis, so that the environment is driven by rumour or gossip, and gossip is given the sanctity of fact. Rumours are what matter, rather than a rational, logical business case built on a true understanding of what is really going on. Skilled people within the organization are denied a voice and so they all despair and leave, as the CEO eventually did.

In contrast, several of our storytellers spoke explicitly about bringing external perspectives into the organization. The first storyteller was seeking to engage her organization in the idea of becoming a retailer rather than a wholesaler:

> The leadership team didn't see themselves as retailers, so I brought some retailers in from outside to help convince the nay-sayers. The people I hired from big-retail brought energy and an understanding of what you needed to do to be successful. It took a while for the leadership team to get used to them, to seek to understand their point of view versus telling them what to do, but in time we all become open to their suggestions and captured their expertise in a broader way.

This storyteller spoke about a method he has used a few times to help the organization think outside the comfortable and familiar:

> I found one or two people who'd worked for the organization previously and persuaded them to come back. These were people who'd experienced the outside world and knew there was another way. I love that model!

This CEO was attempting to build bridges between his organization and an external community of key stakeholders:

We needed to engage with the research community and so I brought someone from that community into our team. It helped us understand what we could do to help them succeed and the value of connecting them with the human consequences of their work.

The burning platform

The 'burning platform' story is a metaphor widely used by change practitioners. The idea is that to effect change we need to persuade people that the oil rig is on fire so that the only option is for everyone to jump into the sea. Sixteen per cent of our storytellers began their stories with scenarios of impending doom – companies on the verge of going bust, or of being taken over, or of being banned from trading – but the metaphor doesn't reflect the process that the rest of our storytellers described. The burning platform metaphor appears to suggest that it's the responsibility of the change leader to identify a critical issue then seek to persuade others of its importance. What we heard from our stories was something different and less sequential, where change is constant and the leader's role is to participate in an ongoing dialogue, funnelling a myriad of views into something that makes sense for the majority. One of our storytellers put it like this:

> The burning platform is exaggerated – you either have one or you don't. It's a rare phenomenon. More often what you have are embers. What you do need is the narrative. At my previous organization we constructed a narrative very carefully and shared it with the workforce through different channels. They were thrilled and energized; at the first presentation they cheered. They'd never been addressed in that way before.

In summary then, the change leader's role is to make sure that people have a common vision toward which they are working. That vision will always be co-created. The question is, have all important perspectives been taken into account in forming the vision? As long as the change leader is committed to the idea that visions change over time as the environment changes, and is committed to ongoing dialogue and regular reflection, then it's unlikely to be catastrophic if early visions don't entirely resonate. Not all employees expect or desire to be involved in an intensive process of co-creation, but they do appreciate being listened to, being acknowledged and being addressed.

This is not the end of the story, however. From dialogue emerges perspective and vision, but even if the change leader succeeds in facilitating a common understanding of perspectives, this doesn't guarantee that people will agree on future vision. Indeed there often emerges real tension between the here-and-now and different perspectives on the future. One of the main sources of that tension is identity, discussed next, in Chapter 8.

KEY POINTS

- We are social beings engaged in a constant network of interactions with others. The visions and insights we have for the future are therefore essentially social in nature. Whether we are aware of it or not, the visions we advocate to others are essentially co-created.

- To recognize that our views for the future are co-created is to position the value of reflecting upon those views. What experiences and perspectives have we been influenced by? What views and perspectives have we not yet sought out? How might those views influence our own?

- Purpose and vision are dynamic and evolve as the environment changes and our understanding of ourselves in that environment also changes.

- One role of the change leader is to keep the dialogue going so that people remain aligned around a common purpose in the face of change. Another role of the change leader is to work out who to engage in visioning, and to think both inside and outside of the organization.

- To rely on 'burning platforms' as a mantra for change means that some changes will be hard to contextualize, and that change is always likely to be predicated on fear.

The evolution of identity

08

The limitations of logic

Beech *et al* (2011) critique the traditional approach to change and the implicit assumption that change is a rational, structured, linear journey. Many change programmes privilege a particular version of reality (Tsoukas and Chia, 2002) assuming it to be the only logical representation of that reality. As the change effort unfolds, others tend to be categorized as 'pro-change' or 'anti-change', a perspective that is based on another set of assumptions: that people's views are fixed and straightforward. This black-and-white assumption doesn't easily allow for the possibility that people's views are in a state of constant flux, that people can hold more than one view at the same time, and people may support some aspects of a proposed change and not others.

If change efforts rarely succeed when based solely on an appeal to logic, what else is there to appeal to? While commending the change leader's role in 'declaring' the desired change in the world, Tsoukas and Chia (2002) distinguish between the expectation that people will then straightaway comply, with the expectation that such a declaration may make it possible for people to see things differently. If I expect people to comply then I am likely to categorize those who ask me questions as 'resistant'. If I believe people ultimately need to make their own sense of events, then I am likely to respect challenge as part of that meaning-making process. We all make sense of things differently, based on our individual and collective experiences and beliefs. In this sense meaning-making is closely linked to identity, such that Thurlow and Helms Mills (2009) suggest that the focus of any change initiative is essentially to redefine identities.

Identity

Consider the following story about an office move:

> We'd been in the same building since the early 1900s. Some people had worked their whole careers in the same building. It wasn't open plan, and the design

reflected the hierarchical way the company operated. The new CEO saw the move as an important part of shifting the culture. To address complaints such as, 'I don't want to change my commute', we moved just round the corner. We involved people in choosing furniture, adopted suggestions on featuring 'quiet rooms' in the layout, allowed people to name meetings rooms and so on. We found we were in fact managing two change processes: one for the newer people, which was all about 'what's in it for me', the second one for those who'd been working for the company for a long time. For them the building and the company were the same thing and they seemed to go through some kind of grieving process. There was something about the move that meant they lost their status as having been around longest. So we managed them differently. We gave them arms and legs to do some of the work required to make the move happen, for example. We also introduced a system for the new cafe where everyone had to have a numbered card to buy coffee. We numbered the cards according to length of service, so the person who had served longest got card number 00001, and so on. In the end the move went well, even if some of the long servers insisted on bringing their old chairs to the new office. It was quite a sight seeing people pushing their old chairs along the street to the new office on moving day.

The logic of this office move wasn't about reducing cost; indeed the new location was more expensive than the old one. The logic was about a culture of working together more collaboratively. But for some of the recipients of this message, the logic wasn't compelling, not because it was unsound, but for them the old building held meaning, something to do with stability, tradition and being recognized for the experience you bring to the organization. Ultimately the company was able to incorporate the needs of those people within the proposed move.

Another storyteller told us about an organization's 'family culture' and how this proved to be an obstacle to achieving commitment to a particular strategy:

It was an uncomfortable time for the organization. They'd bought a competitor brand with the intention of maintaining two distinct brands in the market place, but the distinction got lost such that the acquired brand was sucking the life out of our main brand. The only option was to kill the acquired brand. I dedicated a lot of energy to telling the story so that everyone understood. The problem was that killing the brand meant closing down some parts of the business. The organization thought of itself as a family, and families don't ask people to leave. We had to ask some people to go and the organization found that very difficult to cope with, including the owner.

Again, the logic of the proposed change was compelling, but logic wasn't enough. The leadership of the organization saw themselves as the custodians of a 'family' with obligations to members of that family. The change leader couldn't ignore the story of 'organization as family' nor the company owners' identities as patriarchs.

Identity and sense-making

Fifty-four per cent of the people we spoke to referred to the need to understand and address issues of identity and sense-making in orchestrating effective change. Weick *et al* (2005) define sense-making as a retrospective process by which people rationalize the events of the past. People engage intensely in sense-making at times of change, when effort is required to find order in chaos. People look for the story that best fits events, the story that is most plausible. In determining whether a particular interpretation of events is most plausible, people tend to look beyond the logic of that interpretation.

I worked at a retail bank for a while. The bank, like some other banks, asked its staff to look out for opportunities to cross-sell. In other words, if I come in to make a deposit, the staff will take the opportunity to check if I might be interested in taking out a loan, or investing the money in a long-term high interest account, or in buying insurance. The logic for this change seemed compelling; evidence shows that if you proactively suggest that the customer buy a certain product, the customer is more likely to buy that product. In theory the customer is happier, because he is now able to buy that new car, earn more interest or feel safer, and the bank makes more profits.

Persuading frontline staff to change their behaviours, however, proved challenging. Some staff aligned themselves with the bank's logic and began cross-selling without further question. Other staff interpreted the request differently. Some prided themselves on being friendly and supportive, easy to talk to and keen to please. For some of these staff cross-selling meant trying to sell customers products they hadn't asked for. It meant placing the needs of the bank ahead of the needs of the customer, something that clashed with their perception of themselves as individuals, and more importantly with their perception of the organization for which they worked. This alternative perspective was reinforced each time they experienced first-hand a customer expressing displeasure at being 'sold to' instead of engaging in a conversation about the weather, or being served fast with the minimum of fuss. The staff member who was happy to on-sell remembered the times when customers took the opportunity to buy something they hadn't thought of buying and thanked him for his initiative. The staff member with a different perception of himself and the bank remembered the times when customers were less happy. The second group of staff felt worse upon being told by management that their perspective was 'wrong'. Instead of feeling 'guided' they felt they were not listened to, and the bank's apparent unwillingness to listen reinforced the role of the bank as 'rapacious profit-monger' in the story they had begun to write to rationalize the recent sequence of events. For the unhappy bank staff, being asked to cross-sell didn't resonate with how they saw themselves, either as individuals or as members of their organization. These staff voiced their disquiet with other colleagues, seeking their help in trying to work out what the change meant. If sufficient other people were of a similar mind, then they co-created a narrative that both explained the events and suited their view of the world and their role within it. To further scaffold this story, the co-creators of this narrative actively looked for stories that confirmed it, and labelled others in the story according to the role they appeared to be playing.

Sense-making and identity are linked. Sense-making is a process, while identity is a relatively enduring, grounded sense of what makes us different from others. It is therefore very hard to know how people will make sense of a particular initiative without having a good sense of their identity. This provides us with a great loop back to 'listening', in that the effective change leader will be deeply curious, not only about what other people are saying and meaning but also in seeking to understand what underlies that agenda – the other's *identity*.

Collective identities

Our storytellers recounted many stories in which the organization and/or its stakeholders appeared divided into 'coalitions' (Rodgers, 2007) comprised of people with collective identities different to other parts of the organization. Even when such coalitions came to understand each other's perspectives, this didn't mean that they straightaway united on a common purpose. To bring such groups together requires a commitment to engage in dialogue and some form of leadership to make sure all parties feel heard.

The leader of a post-merger global rebranding project shared the following story about bringing together the leadership of lots of heritage organizations with different histories and values. Through dialogue they succeeded in aligning around a single new purpose without being asked to walk away from their respective collective identities:

We were coming out of a period where the company had completed a series of mergers and acquisitions. Each of these companies had their own brand and identity, and we wanted to emerge from that as something different, something better. The CEO wanted people to be proud of the company, wanted it to be something special. We had some fantastic sessions with the MDs, people from the different companies based all over the world. Ultimately the decision was made at one of those meetings, which then gave us the mandate to move ahead, with each entity letting go of parts of its past for the sake of something better in the future.

This next story came from a senior leader asked to take over the back office accounting function for the Asia Pacific division of a global business. He was charged with combining the back office functions across the region, which meant shifting some of the work from Tokyo to Sydney. It transpired that the staff in Tokyo had different opinions from those in Sydney as to what was important. Yet the Tokyo and Sydney staff succeeded in engaging in dialogue. While not everyone ultimately signed up to the proposed change, people felt respected and relationships were preserved:

I had little exposure to Japanese culture, and was tasked with finding out why we hadn't made it work. I had two people in Australia working with the Japanese team; one was a Japanese speaker and the other was an amazing people person. They worked it very gently. The message was that we wanted to focus future growth in the Sydney centre, not close the Tokyo centre in favour of Sydney. We didn't rush. There was a prevailing sense in Japan that the work could only be done properly in Japan. Their biggest fear was that we wouldn't do things to the same standard or be able to communicate with people in Japanese. There was a very low tolerance to people not being able to speak Japanese. First we focused on lower risk activities and moved some of those. We also hired some Japanese expatriates in Sydney, which negated concerns around language and quality and greatly helped overcome some of the resistance. Then we took out some contractor work and the results proved themselves. We hit a block when we wanted to transfer the work of seven of the accounts payable team to Sydney, where the work would be done by four people. The issue was that Japan reconciled the accounts every day, which wasn't necessary. In the end we got the results we needed. Did everyone in Japan say everything worked well? No. Two people resigned because they didn't want to report to someone based in Sydney who was more junior than their manager in Japan. This represented an unacceptable diminishing of status, but the two who resigned still came to dinner and drinks with me after without tension. In the end we won a grudging acceptance that we could do the work equally well out of Sydney.

Multiple identities

Social identity theory (Bond and Seneque, 2012) and self-categorization theory (Hogg and Terry, 2000) suggest that identity formation happens at multiple levels. So we have identities as members of the human race, as male/female, as American, European and so on. Self-categorization theory says that people call upon certain identities in certain situations. So I may act out my role as male parent at home, middle-class European on holiday, and customer advocate when working at the bank. This adds another layer to the idea of what it means to be 'resistant' to change in that as an employee suddenly asked to cross-sell I may feel torn between multiple identities. My identity as a member of a branch team, where we are all uncomfortable with the required change, may not sit comfortably with my role as aspiring leader, keen to engage with the intentions of senior management, or my role as company shareholder, keen to see the values of my share portfolio increase in value.

Identities are co-created

As discussed in Chapter 7, many western societies are highly individualistic. When we think of appealing to people's 'identities' therefore, this may conjure up images of having to travel around the organization appealing to each and every individual separately. Not only would this take a long time, but it is unlikely to be a particularly fruitful approach to engagement. Indeed Burnes (2004) suggests that it is ultimately pointless to focus on changing the behaviour of individuals, because the individual doesn't act in isolation, but is always subject to his relationships with others.

This is consistent with the idea that our identities are co-created. This may feel deeply disempowering to those of us who believe in individual power and control. Reissner (2010) defines identity as our core sense of meaning, the meaning that helps us to reduce anxiety at times of change. In deciding upon our response to change, it is comforting to believe in the sanctity of our own personal values and beliefs, an internal grounding point that helps guide us at times of uncertainty, helps us to find a response that sits comfortably with our sense of who we are as individuals with clear boundaries.

Yet most of us respond to uncertainty by testing our responses with others. We look to others to help us decide what sense to make of events, what to do next, and what implications those actions have in terms of who we are. This isn't to say that we are passive recipients of our identities, it is only to concede that others have a role to play in the evolution of our identities, and that we have a role to play in the ongoing evolution of other's identities, as we all continue to review who we think we are through the events of our lives. Stacey (2012) phrased it thus:

> The silent conversation, of each individual and their public interactions can be thought of as themes and variations reproducing history. It is these themes and variations that organize an individual's experience in the living present. However, what those particular themes are at particular moments will depend just as much on the cues being presented by others as upon the personal history of a particular individual. Each individual is simultaneously evoking and provoking responses from others so that the particular personal organizing themes emerging for any one of them will depend as much on the others as the individual concerned. Put like this, it becomes clear that no one individual can be organizing his or her experience in isolation because they are all simultaneously evoking and provoking responses in each other.

In the first story outlined above, the leadership of each of the heritage organizations engaged in ongoing dialogue to make sense of the proposed move to one brand. Between them they decided how the new brand made sense in the context of their identity as a separate entity with its own tradition and history. From those dialogues emerged renewed narratives about their own separate identities and the emergence of an overarching identity to which they eventually committed. The Tokyo and Sydney accounting teams engaged in dialogue comparing and contrasting their respective senses of what was important and not so important, further building on both their identities as separate teams and the emerging identity of becoming part of a single international accounting organization.

Identity in action

To summarize, traditional approaches to change may assume that people have fixed, individual identities that prevail across multiple contexts. The task of the change leader is then to appeal to all of the different identities in the organization through the one universal language that ought to appeal to all, namely logic. In contrast we are exploring a view here that says we all navigate our way through life with reference to an identity or set of identities, a sense of self. These identities are *not* fixed since every action we take is in effect an identity test.

For example, suppose part of my identity is a belief in being honest and open. According to the story I tell about myself, I always respond frankly when asked a direct question. Imagine I am unexpectedly approached by a peer who asks me for feedback and, in the moment, I hear myself prevaricating such that I walk away having mostly avoided expressing my true observations. My actions don't appear to fit the story. I may feel compelled to revisit the story. Perhaps I choose to redefine myself as honest, truthful and above all considerate. It's likely I will test a few versions of this reinterpretation with others. I may seek help, engaging someone in dialogue to help decide what sense to make of what happened and what conclusions to draw. Though I may not always accept another's interpretations of events, still they have an impact. If, for example, I test with my wife the idea that I am above all considerate and she responds by pointing out how I always forget our wedding anniversary, this may cause me to reflect and look again for a narrative that better fits events.

Creativity has only quite recently resurfaced in my life as an aspect of my identity. When I was a child I wrote stories and drew pictures, but didn't get the sense this was particularly valued by others. Then when I was leaving university I applied for a job with a well-known multinational organization. I was invited to participate in a two-day assessment process. I felt vulnerable, going up against other graduates from a business background, when my degree was in psychology, so I determined to play the role of what I imagined a business person was supposed to be. When they asked me, for example, what I would do were I to suddenly be bestowed a large sum of money, I talked about stocks and shares and savings accounts. At the end of the process I wasn't offered a role. When I asked for feedback I was told that I didn't appear to them to be sufficiently creative. That feedback stayed with me for a long time. In my corporate life I focused on the contribution I could make through the application of logic and rational argument, an approach that may have been reinforced by the narrative of those around me. But I kept writing stories. It wasn't until someone asked to publish one of those stories that I revisited my 'creativity' and attempted to sift through the ongoing process of co-creation through which I had decided that I wasn't creative.

People talk about glass ceilings in the corporate world, often with reference to gender. In my own experience there is another glass ceiling that is based on the identity of 'doer'. I have coached lots of people at or around general manager level wondering how to further progress their careers. The same people often work long hours, getting things done, making sure that their teams are producing good outputs. When faced with the challenge of letting go of some of the detail and focusing on more 'strategic' issues, this can present a real dilemma. Not necessarily because the person is inherently drawn to working on the detail, but because this is a strategy that has helped him to become successful, an approach that is implicitly encouraged by senior management in their desire for a regular flow of high quality outcomes. These people may be admired for their capacity to deliver such outcomes, but this is not always a reputation that helps people get promoted. The biggest barrier to progress often lies within. How does someone who has progressively become identified, by himself and others, with 'getting things done' rework his view of himself to someone who is more strategic, who takes the long view and who delegates work to others?

Meaning-making and identity evolution are social. Further, we are saying that we don't have just one identity, but multiple identities, at least one of which is likely to be the 'me' who goes to work, an identity specific to the work environment, the evolution of which others contribute to through their words and deeds.

Giving and receiving feedback

Thinking about the world from this perspective may help us understand why giving and receiving feedback can be so challenging. Receiving feedback is a confronting experience for many people. To be told I am a poor communicator, for example, may not be so simple as to hear I need to communicate better. If I am holding onto a previously scribed story that says I communicate well, that effective communication is a key attribute of any half-decent leader, and that as a 'people-person' communication is one of the things I do best, then I am not just being asked to change a behaviour; I'm being asked to rewrite who I am. Most of us don't like our identities to be threatened. We like our identities to feel stable and constant. We like to feel that no matter how ambiguous or mysterious the events in the outside world, our inner worlds remain stable and predictable. We like to think of ourselves in terms of enduring values and beliefs. We like the idea of being true to ourselves, of being resolute and dependable. It is comforting to think of ourselves as being boundaried entities, separate from the outside world (Reissner, 2010).

Giving feedback can be equally challenging, especially if I am prone to expressing my feedback through the lens of my own narrative. If, for example, I experience a direct report express herself stutteringly in front of a large audience, and I am holding on to a story that says to speak hesitatingly in front of others means the person is lacking in confidence and will find it tough to ever become an influential leader, then instead of couching my feedback solely in terms of the behaviour I witnessed, I am likely to lace my feedback with my own interpretation of that behaviour. 'You stumbled over your words' becomes 'you are a poor communicator and lack confidence'. Not surprisingly, feedback delivered in this way may invoke strong emotional reactions, because I am imposing my interpretation onto another instead of giving them space to make sense of events in a way that may feel more empowering. After a few experiences of finding themselves confronted with strong emotion it isn't surprising if people just stop giving feedback, or that people may be unwilling to receive feedback.

One of our storytellers told how he ensured the delivery of feedback very effectively in a scenario where it could all have gone very wrong. He was working in China at the time, managing a big property development:

> I spoke no Mandarin and the head of the construction company spoke no
> English, but he was critical to the success of the venture. His girlfriend turned
> up at the office one day with a gift to express his appreciation. It was a $35,000
> watch. I knew how much it cost because they left the receipt in the box. I took it
> to the CFO and told him I was sending it back, but I had to be very careful. My
> first instinct was that it was an attempt to bribe me, but I knew things worked
> differently in China. I got my assistant to speak to them. She said all the right
> things so as not to offend. She said that the value of our relationship was worth
> far more than the watch or something like that. Whatever she said worked and
> the relationship stayed strong.

Pace

The purely logical perspective is often an impatient one. It's about demonstrating the evident 'truth' of the change leader's perspective and moving quickly to the execution of the plan. Looking at change from the 'identity perspective' it becomes more obvious why time is often required. It takes time to develop hypotheses as to how a new way of behaving might sit well against the person I think I am, the team to which I belong and the organization I think I work for. I want to reflect on the idea, throw some hypotheses out to my trusted colleagues and hear what they have to say. If I find myself becoming comfortable with the idea, or at least ambivalent, I may want to experiment with the new behaviour and see how it feels, and what impact it has on others. My first experiment may not go so well, such that I want to reflect again and engage in more dialogue. This is a process that takes time, often in a world that prizes action and delivery. Several of our storytellers spoke about their efforts to manage their patience, or the patience of other stakeholders. This leader told the story of efforts to regionalize accounting functions:

> Patience and perseverance were key. We were there every eight weeks, building trust. It was important to have someone on our team who was sympathetic to the Japanese perspective. I had one person on my team who had lived there for eight or nine years. I had someone else on the team for a while who worked well in Australia, but didn't go so well working with the Japanese team. He was a huge fan of his guy in Japan, but he mishandled him. The Japanese guy was intelligent and had great language skills. He was very cosmopolitan, but he was also rigid. The Australia-based guy cared about his Japanese team but was also of the opinion that Sydney was calling the shots and that the guys in Japan should accept that and just get on with it. The pace of the transition really frustrated him. He thought they should do as they were told. However, getting the buy-in was fundamental, and it was grudging and slow.

The next storyteller became CEO of a chain retailer after it was acquired by a private equity company. He remained in charge after it was acquired by a large grocery retailer and recognized the need to allow for time for the two organizations to find a way to work together, respecting their different histories and ways of working:

> The first year was hard and I felt the pressure, but we just had to soldier along. After we were sold, the journey continued. I was careful to spend time understanding our new owners. We were a second-class citizen there, but I made sure we were politically correct. They already had a brand operating in the same market as us, and were trying to do in that brand what we had already done, which meant we had to soak up a barrage of communications and mandates. Again, I had to be patient, take it figuratively and translate the outcomes they wanted into actions that would work in our business. It just took patience.

The following storyteller watched one of his direct reports successfully manage the global rollout of a new procurement system. He remarked how impressed he was at the amount of effort the person put in to creating time to interact with internal stakeholders:

> It was a mammoth project and required persistence. Typically he involved people well before a rollout, doubling the amount of time he spent engaging them. All this psychology! It wasn't the technical complexity. I used to think you could accelerate human change, now I'm not sure you can. I think there's a time period over which people have to absorb information and get used to the

change. It takes quite a while, in this case nine months. I've seen big projects implemented fast, and fail.

This internal practitioner talked about the lessons he had learnt from implementing a series of large change programmes over several years, including the need to manage pace:

> Never give up. Meet with resistors. Have a fall-back. Someone who really wants to drive change just has to get on with it and accept it won't go as fast as you'd like. Eventually more and more people join in. People will join at their own pace and that's fine. The problem usually comes from within yourself – impatience. It can't be run by marching soldiers all at the same pace.

Some storytellers found they tried to push too hard, too quick:

> I thought I could do it overnight, but I couldn't. It couldn't be logicked out. Richard Goyder at Wesfarmers talked about the decision to buy Coles. He said it would take seven years and that he expected to be caned by the staff and the market. He said it would take a wholesale change in people over time. I should have had a four- or five-year plan. I should have got others involved. I started off OK but then I got impatient. The water cooler conversation became very nasty.

This storyteller was a senior manager in a large police force. He told stories about both pushing too hard and creating the time to manage the process more effectively:

> We were re-evaluating everyone's jobs. It was framed as a simple process: we just looked at all the job descriptions, scored them and then sent out letters to everyone telling them the outcome. People walked off the job. There were protests and lots of negative publicity. We realized that if someone got murdered right at that moment, we wouldn't have had anyone to send to the scene. We failed to appreciate the people impact. Deadlines became important, but we missed the point. We were ticking boxes on a Gantt chart and not having the difficult conversations. Some of us raised concerns, but the Chief Constable was unmoved. Hierarchy overcame sensible decision making. Deadlines became more important than listening to the voices that were raising concerns. Six years later I was poised to lead a whole system change impacting on pay and conditions. I recognized the importance of opening the system up and giving people the opportunity to explore options and ideas. I wanted to create the space for challenging and opposing. Despite the pressure I created a four–five month space to work with the top team and help them to understand themselves in service of being able to go out and hold a dialogue across the organization.

The alternative

The traditional approach to change is more directive. According to the traditional model the change leader's task is to create a sense of urgency about a particular outcome, then 'communicate, communicate, communicate' to persuade the organization of the importance of taking steps to achieve that outcome. This somewhat behaviourist approach suggests watching for first signs of compliance, then celebrating the success of those first steps, so assuring others that this is the direction to take. This is in essence an autocratic model for change in which there is little room for dissonance or pushback. This is the kind of narrative in which we find reference to 'burning platforms'. One of our storytellers told the story of such an intervention that may be said to have been successful:

> The company was subjected to a material fine by an industry regulator which was promptly followed by media attention. Responding to the crisis required making radical changes to an organization that was deeply entrepreneurial with staff enjoying significant bonuses. We needed to create change in terms of behaviours and a control infrastructure under the banner of a 'compliance culture'. If we hadn't satisfied the regulators and our board then we would have run the risk of being shut down. An external consultant conducted a review of our culture and structure and came up with a list of recommendations we needed to implement to satisfy all stakeholders. We then created a number of projects to implement the changes. The case for change was understood: we needed to create a compliance culture. We harmonized everyone's performance contract, including the CEO, mapping items in those contracts to the projects. We drove the programme systematically, shining a light on what was wrong and fixing it. We ticked off each item as we implemented it, publicizing the achievement of each one. In the middle of the project the underlying business performance dropped off and certain staff became disgruntled, with a few leaving because the fun was gone. The organization inevitably became more bureaucratic but people were still able to do deals. Some people said we went too far, others were doubters, seeming to think the organization would revert back to what it was if they ignored what was happening. It was tough. It was about staying the course, being boring, and not getting knocked off.

In the event the organization achieved what it set out to achieve. A whole new set of policies and procedures were implemented across the business that saved it from being closed down by the regulators. The process was successful because the person leading the change stuck to his guns, showed great qualities of perseverance and resilience, and had the unwavering support of his line management. Success came at a cost, however, with people leaving the organization and others feeling disengaged working as part of a less commercial and more bureaucratic culture. In this instance, however, there appears to have been little option. Performance suffered, but the alternative was going out of business. This may be an example of an autocratic hierarchical approach to change being an effective strategy, but it's unlikely to provide desired outcomes for organizations seeking change in other contexts where the continuing engagement and retention of staff are seen as possible and desirable.

Values

Discussion of 'identity' may resonate most in a discussion of corporate values. Most organizations have corporate values. They are posted on walls, sometimes built into performance agreements and feature in shareholder publications. The creation of values is usually facilitated by a core team, often OD professionals, on behalf of the senior executive. The conversation is often aspirational and driven by the desires of the senior executive as to how they would like everyone to be behaving. The communication of these values (usually monologic) is accompanied by a description of how people should hold each other to account for these behaviours, including how people can gain/lose financially as a consequence of being formally evaluated.

This kind of approach isn't really a dialogue about values so much as a monologue about desired behaviours. The communication of the new values is in effect a mandate from the top of the organization to the bottom, saying: 'This is how we would like you to behave, so that we can tell our shareholders and customers that this is how they can expect you to behave.' In practice some people comply and others don't, depending on the extent to which management processes are able to monitor and measure day-to-day behaviours.

An organization's true identity is a consequence of the dialogue that takes place between its members on an ongoing basis. As such an organization's identity is neither generic, uniform nor constant. To attempt to capture the essence of the organization's values or identity is an imprecise exercise, a fuzzy snapshot taken at a point in time. What we can be sure of is that efforts to tell organizations what their identities should be will usually be ineffective, sometimes dramatically so. The following story comes from a senior executive working inside a global multinational. She was invited one day to a hotel in London, together with 500 other executives from across the globe.

> I was one of a group of executives invited to a hotel to attend the launch of the new brand values. The CEO stood on the platform and told us all what the new values were. There was a complete rebellion and he was left standing there looking embarrassed, unsure what to do. The list was very long, too long to remember – and what did the words mean? It was ill-conceived, the opposite of getting everyone's point of view. It was a very poor example of how to manage such a process. It wasn't genuine and whatever happened next was bound to be met with scepticism.

The organization's response to being presented with values is usually more circumspect. The declaration of an organization's values is treated like any other top-down monologic communication. Some people may feel immediately engaged with the values espoused, either because the values are similar to their own, or else because they have values related to hierarchy and compliance. Others are more likely to wonder, what next? What do these values really mean? What relevance do they have in everyday working life? People will share their questions with each other as they attempt to make sense of the missive, and watch leaders in the organization to see what they do, seeking clues in their behaviour. Often there is very little change in behaviour. What happens instead is that people at all levels of the organization rationalize their existing behaviours with reference to the new values.

Dialogue and identity

Like perspective and purpose, identity is both an input to, and consequence of, dialogue. The change leader who attempts to drive through an agenda without dialogue is likely to meet with resistance even if the message has been clearly thought through and articulated. An absence of dialogue means that the leadership of the organization are unlikely to be aware of what the rest of the organization is thinking and feeling: what sense they have made of recent events, what sense they make of the present, or what hopes they have for the future. The change leader's message may be both logical and articulate, but if it doesn't address what matters, it is likely to be heard as being irrelevant and/or implausible.

By participating in dialogue, the change leader becomes more informed as to other's perspectives and hopes for the future, and facilitates the same process in others. Whether or not all of these perspectives fit with the change leader's perspective, the change leader is nevertheless able to craft a message more likely to come across as plausible. The change leader is also able to sense-*give*, to play an active role in helping people make sense of changing events (Werkman, 2010).

Through dialogue the change leader may also develop a better understanding of identity, the experiences, beliefs and values that underpin what people say and feel. Organizations have multiple identities: a complex, shifting set of individual and team identities and a sense of how the organization as a whole sees itself. People bring their identities to dialogue, and identity acts as a filter through which people view events and hear other's interpretations of those events.

It is in this sense that Thurlow and Helms Mills (2009) suggest that the focus of any change initiative is essentially to redefine identities. The sensemaking process is often about finding a new sense of identity, a new narrative, a new story that defines us and our teams and organizations and the relationships between these different entities. The effective change leader engages in dialogue with an authentic sense of curiosity, for if he expects others to be open to a new sense of self, then he too needs to be open to the possibility that his own identity may undergo a shift as a consequence of that change.

KEY POINTS

- People are rarely persuaded to engage in change purely by logic and rational analysis.

- We all have a sense of who we are as people. Indeed we have multiple identities; me as leader, me as parent, me as partner, etc. Moreover, we adopt collective identities as the members of teams and organizations.

- Change often has an implication for one or more of our identities. However much work has been done in helping people to achieve a common perspective of the present, if the proposed change has implications for our identity, we may need time to work that out. As part of working it out we are likely to seek to engage in dialogue with others. If a request for dialogue is met with monologue then we'll seek others more willing to engage.

- We take our identities into dialogue and attempt to make sense of change with reference to those identities. If we are successful, we may leave the dialogue having changed the way we think about ourselves in relation to others; we may have experienced a subtle identity-shift.

- The most important task of a change leader is not so much getting people to agree with a detailed outcome as to help different groups of people with different group identities find their own way to align with a broader purpose.

- If we attempt to gain other's compliance with change without engaging them in dialogue we are likely to meet resistance. The resistance is likely to feel mysterious if we have an overwhelming belief in the power of logic and/or haven't engaged in dialogue to attempt to understand the needs of different parts of the organization.

- It is only through dialogue, as opposed to monologue, that we can help others make sufficient sense of a desired change such that they emerge from the process energized and committed.

PART THREE
Power and politics

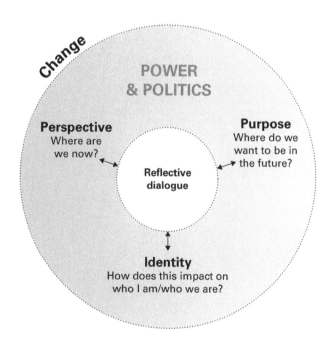

Power and politics

09

Power shows up in two guises in much of the change literature. In its most common incarnation it appears as the primary means through which change is effected. This often implicit reference to power sits behind many of the traditional models of change in which the agenda is determined by people at the top of a hierarchy whose role it is to then persuade the rest of the organization to step into line. 'Resistance to change' often refers to the apparent unwillingness of the recipients of a change message to comply. These approaches to change emphasize the important of clear, logical, sustained one-way communication.

In its second guise power shows up, paradoxically, as absent. Many of these models emphasize the importance of collaboration and the creation of an environment in which everyone can work together respectfully. They make no mention of power, as if power were something to overcome in service of effective collaboration. At a management course recently I read in the hand-out:

> For collaboration to work effectively, power games and politics need to be extinguished. Collaboration has nothing to do with power; it is to do with harnessing ideas, people and their best thinking to find innovative ways to adapt to dynamic conditions. It's the essence of co-creating, creating something together which allows everyone's value to be expressed and respected.

The stories, on the other hand, suggest otherwise. No less than 72 per cent of our storytellers made some mention of power or politics. These are variables that cannot be ignored. As one of our storytellers said: 'Some people say all that matters is the conversation. It's not.' For many people politics is a bad word; it represents an impenetrable web of mysterious relationships inhabited by the unscrupulous and Machiavellian. People who shun politics often say things like, 'I'll just focus on doing a good job and let my record speak for itself,' but power and politics shape our environments. They are present whether we like it or not.

Power refers to the imbalance of control between different people, teams or organizations. These imbalances of control can't be extinguished. Politics is power in action, people exercising their power in overt and covert ways, ways that can be difficult to understand and navigate. Politics is an aspect of complexity, and complexity is hard to navigate by means of logic and rationale alone. Our discomfort with power and politics reflects our discomfort with complexity.

Support from the top

Fifty-six per cent of storytellers said that support from the top is required if change is to be successful. People told me stories where this support was absent and change failed. This internal practitioner, for example, talked about a change programme he was asked to facilitate in South Africa. He engaged first with middle managers in the organization:

> The strategy work started well. People developed a plan inside three months then said they could do it by themselves. Within three weeks it was dead. The top guy didn't really want it; he saw it as challenging his position. The top leader reminded everyone he was the top leader, but he wasn't inspirational and provided no direction-setting. He drove his own area and neglected the rest but didn't allow anyone else to take over.

On the other hand I heard lots of stories about CEOs and MDs successfully leading change. For example:

> The business was losing $10 million a year. He came in as the new CEO and played the role of orchestrator. He changed relationships with key external stakeholders and rebuilt the internal organization, promoting from within, coaching people into more senior roles. He changed the technology platform and the distribution technology, all based on a clear strategy. He saw the potential for it becoming a very different business.

In this story the storyteller reached out to the senior executive to intervene in a programme that may not otherwise have been successful:

> I was trying to implement a new system. I'd done all the right things; I'd shared the vision and the benefits with everyone, and presented it to all the Asian countries. We rolled out successfully in most countries flawlessly, but one country GM didn't want it: Singapore. I couldn't work out why, and wondered if it was for personal reasons. I couldn't get to the bottom of it; all I got was a

lot of excuses. Singapore was an important milestone for us and if that hadn't gone ahead, the rest of the rollout could have been endangered. Ultimately I elevated it to the global CFO who contacted the VP Finance in Singapore and told him to implement the system – or else. You can have all the best practice in place, but if there are resisters then they may need to be taken to the brink.

This CEO took his business to the brink with the support of his global executive:

I knew that I would have to make big changes to the executive team if I was going to be successful. I changed 60 per cent of the team. It was a big step but it worked. At the same time I got a new boss. He told me I was mad, to which I responded that we were in a world of trouble and we needed to do something drastic. It was too late for him really to do anything about it and he told me: 'You've done it now. I'll support you and let's see how you go.'

These stories tell us that the support of the senior leader will often be required if change is to be successfully implemented. This doesn't mean that support from the top is sufficient.

The limitations of positional power

Consider the following story, again from South Africa. This external practitioner told the story of a mining organization in Johannesburg that committed to transform the way the company operated and contributed to the transformation of the local community. Hundreds of thousands of people in that community lived in shanty towns where there were high levels of unemployment and crime. The organization embarked on a whole raft of projects involving thousands of employees and people from the community. The programme ultimately failed:

My sense was that some of the white South Africans didn't behave with integrity. They saw the MD was committed and went along because they saw they had to be seen to be not racially discriminating against others. They complied, but when the going got tough their underlying lack of commitment became evident. If something didn't work it was because 'the blacks can't handle it'. You have to have people truly committed or else move some people out. Ninety per cent of the supervisors were white South African and I don't think 70 per cent of them were totally committed. There wasn't enough attention paid to that. We hoped they'd become more supportive, and some did, but many were too embedded in the old Afrikaner mindset. To give that up would have been giving up who they were. They went to workshops, they went to meetings, but when things got tougher... There have to be people looking for those issues.

An internal practitioner from Europe spoke about the transformation of a global manufacturer/distributor of a well-known branded range of products:

We had tried centralizing functions before. It was clear that we needed to: the organization had grown four times in size through acquisitions over ten years. The old structure in which the operating companies drove everything wasn't working and we needed a new business model. The problem was that local management in the operating companies were the kings in the old structure and so they pushed back on the idea of centralizing because they felt threatened. We tried before and failed, officially because the business case didn't stack up, but in reality it was largely because of line manager resistance.

When disciplinary power is relied upon as the sole strategy by which to push change down through an organization, not only is the immediate change unlikely to be successful, but the capacity of the organization to later exercise power if it is offered becomes diminished. One of our storytellers talked about going to lead a business in an Eastern European country:

The population is well educated, but since the political changes in the early 1990s they have struggled with political uncertainty and a challenging financial environment. Broadly speaking, organizations continue to be hierarchical and people are still adapting to be held accountable and being asked to make decisions for themselves. The organization I joined was still quite bureaucratic and decisions were made at the top. When I arrived the team wanted me to tell them the answers and when I told them it wasn't me who was going to decide, that it was them, they looked nervous. Every senior manager before you, they said, has told us what to do, which was to cut costs rather than try and find a way to make the business effective.

None of this is to suggest there is no room for disciplinary power. Stacey (2012) points out that leaders do have designated power and there are times when it is clearly appropriate to exercise that power, but relying solely on it to drive large-scale change down through an organization is unlikely to work.

The executive team

Thirty per cent of our storytellers spoke about the importance of engaging the whole executive team. This external practitioner told the story of a managing director in Asia who committed wholeheartedly to a change effort. He succeeded in engaging parts of the broader organization but he didn't succeed in getting his own management team on board:

> The new CEO asked me to help him get the whole organization aligned around a new vision. I suggested he test his intent with the leadership team; if they were on board he had a chance, otherwise he'd end up alone. We did a diagnosis – interviews and focus groups etc – collated the data and shared it with the leadership team. The leadership team's language was all external; they weren't owning it. I played their language back to them, but they still didn't fully engage. The CEO, on the other hand, was an integral part of the process. He exuded phenomenal energy. He dropped by the change office on a regular basis and talked to people. He showed an unparalleled level of commitment. The rest of the leadership team came only when invited, more out of obligation than genuine interest. The CEO left it up to them. He talked about picking our battles and questioned if their support was essential. He wanted to nudge them into taking an interest and thought if we got one of them on board we'd get the rest. In the end the project was a modest success. Not getting the whole of the leadership team passionate and on board was our biggest failure. As a consequence they demarcated their functional agendas from the big change agenda, which meant too many people found it hard to get involved.

The cohesion of the executive team was another aspect of the South African story recounted earlier in this chapter:

> The CEO made a personal commitment to transforming the way in which the company operated and to making a contribution to the transformation of South African society. We involved people across the business, the unions and local communities, and formed a charter, which then led to lots of projects and initiatives rolled out to tens of thousands of people. It got underway but there were lots of issues and it wasn't successful. One of the key learnings for me was you have to have that foundational leadership from the executive team. They need to represent their areas and be prepared to apply everything they know to make it a success. They need that emotional and rational commitment at a deep level. If not then the leader at the top has to be prepared to move them away. You can't have people not totally committed.

This leader, on the other hand, made sure he had the right team in place to manage a complex programme of business restructuring:

> It was a big effort and it took a long time. We needed people who would get it done effectively. I inherited a team in which some roles were filled by

enthusiastic amateurs. I needed experts and hired them in. When you're in the middle of complexity you see all the barriers; it's hard to sit in the middle of a reincarnation, and people may feel it can't be done. I brought in fresh faces, people who knew how to get the job done. Then we started tackling some of the real problems.

Middle management

Forty-four per cent of storytellers spoke more broadly about empower-ment, with several talking specifically about the importance of involving middle management. I heard about change initiatives that 'crashed upon the rocks' of middle management, and I heard terms such as 'frozen middle' to describe the apparent inertia of middle management amid change. Top-down approaches to change can easily disempower middle management, with failure being the consequence:

> Up until that point we had a real change of mood. Middle management
> was very committed – 'We can do it!' Then they brought in the consultants.
> The consultants were all dynamic and strong and they overrode the middle
> management layer. I went there every four weeks and each time I visited I saw
> ownership being progressively given up and people becoming demotivated. The
> consultants were imported from another restructuring play. They introduced all
> their models and practices with good intentions, but they disengaged people.
> These were people who'd started to own their own destiny. Step by step they got
> pushed back into minor roles, delivering data and doing what they were told.

The CEO of a well-known retailer expressed similar misgivings about dis-empowering middle managers from implementing change:

> We didn't employ any consultants or external people. Our logic was that we
> can be change agents, but you need people who understand the business to
> help you make the change. The idea people can't change generally isn't true;
> it depends on the environment and the objectives you give them, the support
> you give them. They knew how to get things done, versus smart consultants.
> It's consistency of application that's important, not speed. The journey may
> take years. In a good turnaround you manage the broad themes; the dynamics
> change continually. Consultants can forget the need to hit the numbers. They
> write nice theoretical plans but you can't sack everyone at once. Operators can
> be too focused on the numbers though, so you need balance. You must talk to
> people, get to know what inspires people, set some objectives, achieve one, and
> build some momentum.

The support of the senior executive is therefore important in the success of any change programme but is unlikely to be sufficient; the senior team need to enrol middle management. I get the sense that many top executives intuitively realize this, which may explain the reluctance of some top executives to drive a change programme forward the way they are being asked to by change managers who apparently believe in the sanctity of positional power.

The middle management layer is often the point at which monologue ceases to be effective and dialogue is essential. The CEO or MD may have had the opportunity to hand-pick a team of like-minded people with similar experiences, beliefs and aspirations, a team who spend a lot of time together generating a common perspective in the here-and-now. The further down the organization you go, however, the more difficult it becomes to iron out the wrinkles that diversity brings; people are more likely to work in different locations, deal with different people, live in different communities, belong to different generations. As suggested in Chapter 8, while management may expect unquestioning compliance to a logical/rational argument, people will make their own meaning of all such edicts. If senior management doesn't appear willing to engage in that meaning-making process, through dialogue, people turn to their immediate colleagues. Employees want to hear the message from their local management anyway because they know their local management, and local management is more likely to couch change in terms that can be related to their immediate surroundings (Allen *et al,* 2007).

Thomas and Hardy (2011) write specifically about the interface between senior and middle management, and how effective dialogue between the two levels of management can create new meaning. If, however, senior management chooses to engage in monologue rather than dialogue, and chooses not to respond to questions posed by middle management, eventually middle management will stop talking to senior management. Middle management will keep talking amongst themselves however, and what emerges from that dialogue is unlikely to please senior management. It's at this stage that senior management is likely to label middle management as being 'resistant to change'. At this point the world may become especially unsafe for middle management, particularly if change is likely to involve demotions or dismissals, and the message communicated back up the hierarchy is likely to become compliant, at least on the surface. Middle management may then exercise their power by cooperating to the minimum extent they feel they can get away with, focusing instead on protecting themselves and their turf. Lo and behold we have what one of our storytellers called the 'frozen middle'. If, on the other hand, middle management is engaged in dialogue and is empowered, this layer of management has the potential to act as a crucial facilitator of change (Raelin and Cataldo, 2011). Conway and Monks (2011) say that middle managers must be empowered if they are to be able to implement change in their own areas. Managers need to be 'the first targets of empowerment and involvement practices rather than just the implementers of involvement for their subordinates'.

Frontline staff look to middle management, the people they know and sometimes trust, to help them make sense of change. In other words, middle management often has relational power, a power that may need to be leveraged if a change programme is to be successful. This was neatly articulated by one of our storytellers talking generally about his learning from effective change programmes:

> I've learnt about the role of the supervisor. People have to be able to interpret what change means for them and their teams. Team members look to the team leader to verify what it means: is it good or bad? Is it doable or undoable? Supervisors have got to get it. Supervisor commitment is just as important as executive commitment.

One of our storytellers was responsible for occupational safety programmes:

> I don't know why it's proved so difficult to engage our Australian workforce in adopting new safety practices. In the Asian businesses people seem to appreciate being safer and they just get on and do what they're told; in the UK and the US too. In the UK the workforce look out for each other and are alert to how the person next to them is doing their work. In Australia they don't speak up, it's more a case of, 'Give him a go – see how he goes – we'll help him if he gets into trouble.' In Australia there seems to be something in the national identity about 'manning up'; I think it comes from sports like NRL where you are expected to assume a degree of risk. We've tried everything in Australia, but it hasn't worked. My theory is that the supervisors are key; they're the role models and people look up to their team leaders. If you get good behaviours there – that's one avenue. We're about to make some big interventions in supervisor training and see if that works.

Middle managers are thus the recipients *and* purveyors of change. Life often isn't easy for the middle manager. Structural changes may result in cost-cutting and staff reductions, which may not only mean that middle managers are uncertain as to their own futures but also that they may have more work to do in the meantime. Downsizing and delayering means middle management are asked to exercise greater spans of control and do more work, while at the same time they may be experiencing greater job anxiety (McCann *et al*, 2004). Middle management may quickly become disillusioned (Scase and Goffee, 1986), feel isolated (Burke and Cooper, 2000; Scase and Goffee, 1989) and/or experience their identities being threatened (Thomas and Linstead, 2002; Turnbull, 2001). Stories abound of middle management not being successfully engaged in the purpose of change, but expected nevertheless to implement their roles with commitment and enthusiasm even when inadequately empowered and resourced.

Power and politics in practice

In practice engaging the support of middle management and the layers of management below isn't easy. Engaging in dialogue with people takes time. Nor does it guarantee that everyone will necessarily align around a common purpose. Engaging in dialogue facilitates the evolution of shared perspectives, the evolution of organizational identity and the evolution of common purpose, but it serves just as well to facilitate the evolution of informed factions. If we enter into dialogue with the sole expectation that everyone will end up on the same page, then we are not really engaging in dialogue, since we are entering the interaction with a predefined outcome in mind, an outcome that may deafen us to particular perspectives. As I will discuss in Chapters 10 and 12, the outcome of dialogue is sometimes a realization that differences in perspective and vision, often driven by differences in identity, can mean that people are best off going their separate ways.

Fortunately not *everyone* needs to engage around a common purpose for the change to be successful. The effective change leader is aware of the political landscape and charts a path through it, focusing his energies on finding common ground with those who wield most power relevant to the particular agenda. This next leader needed to align an array of different stakeholders working in a Chinese joint venture:

> We were building new real estate just as the real estate market collapsed. We couldn't just turn off our development plans because the Chinese government had already invested in some major infrastructure. We had the government involved, local bodies, government bureaus, mayors, contractors, even the People's Liberation Army. All of them had their own interests, many of them illegal and with which I just couldn't get involved. How did I get things done? First, by becoming good friends with the Chinese contractor and leveraging his power, and second, leveraging the power of my local joint venture partners. I found out that the mainland Chinese people didn't get on with the Hong Kong Chinese, and getting people to make decisions was like moving pieces around a board, very complex. When you meet someone for the first time you need to

work out where that person sits in the bigger picture and work out what to do with that relationship.

The change leader who refuses to 'play politics' may come to regret it. A senior manager told the following story:

> I was expected to persuade the businesses to hand over their services to the new centralized function quickly, and I did, and I got a great performance rating. At the same time my manager told me I had to think strategically, but I couldn't figure out what that meant. Then I wasn't nominated for the top leadership development programme. I didn't find out why but I'm pretty sure someone on the executive said something. Then I did a 360 and found out that my stakeholders said I was a bulldozer and that I wasn't listening to their concerns. I learnt that I should have sought counsel earlier from people who really understood how the organization worked, who were the key people I needed to align with, and that I should have communicated a lot more.

A senior manager told us the story of a systems project that may have contributed to the demise of his CEO:

> His direct reports couldn't agree on which solution was the best and there was a lot of infighting. The CEO didn't want to make an active call; he may have thought – let the best man win, but the noise reached the board who thought it made the CEO look ineffective. One team backed the safe option and the other team backed the supplier who made all sorts of promises. It became evident the risky option wasn't going to work and they withdrew at the last minute, so the team who backed that option changed their view amid a lot of 'I told you sos', yet managed to come out of the whole thing looking as if they had prevailed. The CEO lost his job and the business unit manager running the team who originally backed the risky system was promoted to CEO. There was a lot of money wasted, which all stemmed from not engaging the junior people on the project, who understood the systems better than anyone, but who weren't properly engaged. If they had have been engaged then the whole mess could have been avoided, including the downfall of the CEO.

Power and politics often sit at the heart of the change agenda. This senior manager from South America described how a global organization established a process through which to redesign itself. The process was ultimately successful and involved a great deal of politicking:

> There was a lot of debate and lots of people with different interests. Regional groups wanted more autonomy and the central functions pushed hard for a

centralized model. The owner gave the organization six months to work on structures, with the objective of having two or three different models to present to the board. He nominated nine or ten managers from different countries, regions and functions and we had seven consultants facilitating the process. The group split into two camps and we had long, long debates. For many months we couldn't get breakthrough and it got tense. We spent three days together every week then went home for two days. My boss was very keen to know what was going on and there was a hell of a lot of politicking. I was representing Latin America and another guy was representing France where they only had one small business. Every chance he got he tried to show that France should be independent. People were using the committee to make their personal positions stronger and clear agendas appeared. It was a big problem, but I was doing it too. The French guy was basically trying to make sure he had a job. The German guy was trying to defend having large central departments because otherwise friends of his would lose their jobs. When we went back to our businesses there was more politics there including rebellion against the things we had agreed. The owner was keeping abreast of what was happening along the way and having lots of private discussions with people.

While this process worked in the end, it may not work for everyone given that senior managers were effectively taken out of the business for six months. How else might we successfully navigate the multitude of relationships that make up the political landscape?

Taxonomies, models and tools

There are multiple lenses through which we can view power dynamics; different taxonomies exist. For example Rodgers (2007) lists:

- *Resource power* – the control of resources valued by others.
- *Expert power* – a personal knowledge and expertise relevant to the task at hand.
- *Network power* – a function of the relationships an individual has within an organization.
- *Coercive power* – based on physical or psychological dominance.
- *Symbolic power* – the impact of role-modelling on behaviours and the emergence of meaning.
- *Communication power* – the ability to establish empathy and rapport.

- *Inner power* – a concept similar to the idea of authenticity; the power the authentic individual has in terms of feeling less subject to the thoughts and opinions of others.
- *Relational power* – as exercised through relationships with others.
- *Embedded power* – as defined by formal rules and norms of behaviour.

Some of the stories I heard fitted this taxonomy. This next story sounds like an example of expert power in the context of an organization needing to enhance an old legacy system:

> The system was built in the late 90s and was the core system for the entire business unit. It was developed in-house and just a handful of people remained who knew how it worked. It was a handcuff for the business because it was old and problematic. It was difficult to make changes and some enhancements had to be made to the system due to regulatory changes. We decided to replace the legacy system with an outsourced system, piggy-backing a competitor system, but there was a lot of resistance to even broaching the idea. The legacy system experts picked on functionality that couldn't be replicated and held it up as deal-breakers, or they didn't come to meetings, or they bad-mouthed the executive and the competitor's system. But we needed them until post-migration. So we offered them money to stay even though their behaviour was poor. They had power.

The same storyteller told the story of an office move and an example of some form of power, a mix perhaps of resource and network powers:

> The new office was to be open plan without exception. Lots of people actively fought to retain their offices and we had to ask the CEO to ring people up to tell them they weren't going to get an office. All except the funds managers. They were key, even more important than the CEO. We had to compromise with them. We lost that battle.

A senior manager told the story of being appointed to a senior role in the company's global headquarters, advising one of the group vice-presidents. He found his positional power outdone by relational power:

> When I went to the global head office I didn't read it well. I had a team of three and wanted to get them to work together better. I misread the politics: people have their own agendas and interests. My predecessor wasn't strong and his 2IC (second-in-command), now my 2IC, had taken over. The 2IC wasn't interested in changing the way we worked; he was just interested in maintaining his

relationship with the vice-president, and the vice-president didn't want to piss off the 2IC because he was giving him what he wanted. It took me a while to realize the 2IC had no interest in my success and no interest in supporting the change. I found myself unable to do the job I'd been brought in to do; the VP always asked my 2IC to come to meetings. I learnt that you've got to make sure you know how everyone is linked to the stakeholders, and that you understand the lines of authority and how they work.

These taxonomies and other models and tools may help us think outside the box of positional power but are necessarily simplistic. In any interaction there may be multiple power dynamics at play. The boss talking to her direct report may have more positional power. The direct report, on the other hand, may have more expert power and inner power. The boss may have been at the company longer and have greater network power. These power differentials are dynamic. In a fast changing environment the direct report's expert power may diminish, for example. These dynamics are also context-specific. In certain situations, for example, the direct report may feel less confident and his inner power may not be so prevalent. In a restructure the boss's network may be dissembled and their network power may be reduced. There will be certain situations in which network power may be critical, others in which inner power may be more important. This is the complexity of the power dynamics between two individuals. The power dynamics of an *organization* are much more complex and multi-layered, too complex for us to fully understand and model.

To be attuned to the dynamics of power and politics we need to be listening to what is not being said. We need to stand back and watch how things seem to work, and test our hypotheses by engaging in dialogue with others. For if politics is the exercising of power through interaction then this is where change happens. As Johansson and Heide (2008) put it:

> In sum, power and resistance thus operate together in a web of relations in which power is never complete and possibilities for resistance always exist. Power is exercised through multiple points of pressure and so too is resistance. Such struggles are not necessarily repressive since there is a creative potential when meanings are renegotiated. This conceptualization of power and resistance shifts the focus away from questions of who resists organizational change, why and when, to a question of how relations of power and resistance operate together in producing change, and in what ways.

Using taxonomies and models may therefore be useful in considering the dynamics of an organization, who the key stakeholders are and how to approach them. It may not be so useful if the change leader misuses the model, treating it as if it fully represented the complexity of the organization and the way it works. As Mitchell *et al* (1997) say, there are 'a maddening variety of signals on how questions of stakeholder identification might be answered'. There are many different sources of power, all of which shift and change over time, sometimes slowly, other times fast. We ought to beware those models that purport to help us manage complexity as if it were merely complicated. Network mapping methodologies, for example, may be useful so long as we don't treat their output as factual and complete.

Some of the strategies adopted by our storytellers to manage power and politics appeared to be quite intuitive. For example, this storyteller spoke about going outside the rules to ensure the success of an acquisition in Japan:

> There were rules we were supposed to follow in managing the integration globally: group guidance. In Japan we did things slightly differently. After the integration was complete I was told that you couldn't have both old company names in the new company name. I didn't ask – we just did it and ended up violating the rules. I called it tailoring the guidance of the group to fit our local situation. We need to make sure we integrated the two businesses, but we also needed to make sure local management stayed in place to keep the business profitable.

This storyteller adopted a similar strategy in successfully navigating the needs of different stakeholders:

> We needed to comply with guidance from the group without disempowering our own people. I managed it by taking what the group said figuratively. Tell me what to do and I'll translate it. So when they told us to engage in a particular scheme, which I knew wouldn't work, we made sure we did something to achieve the desired outcome, just a different thing. I just make sure I'm always *directionally* correct.

This storyteller identified two key stakeholder groups with whom he needed to engage and for whom he put in place specific strategies:

> The research community and government are our two most important stakeholder groups. With the research community I brought someone from that community into our team. I recognized we had some stuff that they wanted and we needed their support too. I tried to connect them to the human aspect of our work. Government have a huge bank account and influence our ability to achieve our purpose. At the same time they get beaten up on the economic front,

the human front and the business case front, and so we need to connect with them on all three. So we connected patients with their MPs to explain to them how demanding the disease is. We follow up on the policy positions we think are important and brief them in parliament one by one.

KEY POINTS

- Traditional approaches to change are based on an implicit assumption that positional power is usually the driver behind organizational change. Other approaches to change may emphasize the primacy of dialogue as if power and politics may be ignored.

- Positional power is real, and those with positional power may easily disrupt or put a stop to a particular change. Change may also be disrupted by uncommitted subordinates and whole levels of management who may exercise other forms of power, sometimes passively.

- To succeed in effecting change the change practitioner must survey the power dynamics of the organization and decide how to manage the political terrain. This is strategic and systemic, in that it requires deciding where best to invest one's energies.

- Models and tools can be useful in charting this terrain, so long as the practitioner recognizes that these 'maps' will never be entirely accurate. Power dynamics are often difficult to identify and are constantly shifting and changing.

- The effective change leader makes intuitive decisions based on a judgement in the moment and reviews the success of those decisions on an ongoing basis.

PART FOUR
Themes

Authenticity

10

In this book so far, I've referred directly or indirectly to authenticity on a number of occasions. In Chapter 3 I discussed 'authentic curiosity' in which I suggested that we can only truly listen to what is going on behind the words spoken by another person if we put aside our own agenda for a while and listen with respect to the person before us. I suggested that it's hard to listen to what may underlie people's words and attitudes without first having some awareness of our own beliefs and values. To listen deeply is to be curious and to be aware of the nature of our responses to others.

In Chapter 4 I discussed 'authentic voicing'. I talked about fear as a barrier to speaking openly and honestly; a fear of being challenged for example, or a fear of offending others. Effective voicing requires a degree of confidence in who we are and what we have to say.

In Chapter 5 I talked about reflection, and the propensity of effective leaders to take time out to stand back and views things from a distance. To be reflective is to be curious I suggested, and reflection is a learning process. I talked about the difference between single- and double-loop learning and suggested that to develop a heightened sense of self-awareness entails being open to feedback, indeed hungry for feedback, from others. The desire to learn includes being curious about our emotions, where they come from and what triggers them, both in ourselves and in others.

In Chapter 8 I discussed identity. We learn about ourselves through observing ourselves in action and in engaging in dialogue about those actions. We bring our identities into dialogue, and if we come to dialogue with genuine curiosity we are open to the possibility that our view of ourselves may change as a consequence of that dialogue.

This is not the first book to frame the importance of authenticity in leadership, but we may be framing authenticity differently to some of those texts. In some leadership texts our authentic selves are portrayed as our true selves, a fixed self. The journey to self-awareness is portrayed as a progressive discovery of that fixed self. The authentic leader is the leader who has a good line of sight of that true self and so is able to act from a position of absolute confidence and certainty. To be certain is to be authentic.

The view of authenticity espoused here is different, in that identity and self are seen as being fluid. This is not to say that some aspects of our self don't remain constant over the course of our lives, but other aspects shift and change. There is a sense in which who we are is the story we tell ourselves, and that story changes as we learn more about ourselves through experiencing ourselves as characters in the drama we call our lives.

Think about characters in books. Sydney Carton is a hero because he willingly subjects himself to the guillotine in place of Charles Darnay (Dickens' *Tale of Two Cities*). Winston Smith is ultimately a helpless victim because he betrays his lover (Orwell's *1984*). Lee Child's Jack Reacher is brave and strong because he always confronts the villain. To quote Hollywood screenwriter Robert McKee (1999): 'No matter what they say, no matter how they comport themselves, the only way we ever come to know characters in depth is through their choices under pressure.'

Think of anyone you know well. How do you define who they are? Do you make your decision based on who they say they are, or on what they do? Think of yourself and how you have come to get to know yourself. Just as we learn about others through their actions, so we learn about ourselves through our own actions. The more we act, and the more we reflect upon those actions, the more self-aware we become. If we act without seeking feedback or taking the time to reflect on those actions, then we don't become so self-aware. Some people go their whole lives without finding out much more about who they are because they don't successfully reflect.

As we experience different situations and reflect upon our actions in those situations, so the story we tell about ourselves evolves, so our identities evolve, and as our identities evolve so we make different choices, act differently, and become subtly different versions of ourselves. This is how dialogue and reflection are related to identity, and authenticity defines the extent to which we know ourselves.

Authenticity and identity

Forty-eight per cent of our storytellers spoke about authenticity or self-awareness, and many reflected on their identities during the interviews, sometimes in the guise of their roles or values. This storyteller came from a corporate role into a government organization. This extract of his story is full of identity:

> I was the transformation guy, bringing a modern way of thinking to a
> bureaucratic organization. But the organization's mantra was 'we're a family'
> and I was treated like a drunken Uncle Fester, as an outsider. I was the

'firefighter' rather than the 'architect' or 'builder' and I created some of the bushfires without knowing it. In the second year, when people realized I was a 'glue-man' trying to make everyone successful, I tried to turn relationships round through the use of language. It was hard work, forever selling yourself, always in interview mode. Who are you? What makes you so special, as an ex-private sector person? I assembled my team of 'green berets' to come with me on the journey, and they've all been fantastic.

So this person inhabited the various identities of 'transformation guy', 'architect' and 'builder' while others experienced him as 'drunken Uncle Fester' and 'firefighter' before everyone converged on the co-created identity of 'glue-man'. The next storyteller was the CEO of a retail organization undergoing significant transformation. He played a conscious role within the organization, his identity in that context acting as a clear reference point for his actions:

I knew that successfully playing the role of 'liberator' would be key. I made sure I listened and tapped into to people, making them believe. I played it carefully, releasing the shackles, unlocking the latent energy.

Our next storyteller successfully led a major brand transformation for a global multinational. He was then asked to carry out a very different role, leading the global IT function:

The personal challenge is asking yourself, 'What am I doing here?' I like new companies with a focus on creativity, growth, new opportunities and partnerships, trying to make a difference in the world. That stuff's fun. In the IT job I had aspirations of being more successful than I was. It was mostly an internal focus and saying no. Not fun.

This addresses a fallacy of leadership, that there is a generic leadership template and that people who fit that template will succeed whatever the environment. This leader learnt who he was through doing and now has a story that says he likes to build new partnerships and doesn't like roles with a purely internal focus. This is the identity he now takes into his next experience in the world.

We play with roles and we explore our values. It is only by engaging in life and reflecting upon those engagements that we find out more about these aspects of ourselves. We are, in a sense, both the character in the novel and the reader of the novel, and the reader's impression of the leading character changes as the story told by the book unfolds.

This perspective seems to me to reflect the writings of Viktor Frankl, author of *Man's Search for Meaning*. If we consider identity as that which defines our role in the world, our purpose for even being in the world, then Frankl's words appear to endorse the idea that our identities are fluid and dynamic:

> To invoke an analogy, consider a movie: it consists of thousands upon thousands of individual pictures, and each of them makes sense and carries a meaning, yet the meaning of the whole film cannot be seen before its last sequence is shown.

Courage

Twenty-six per cent of our storytellers spoke of the importance of courage. This CEO told a story about the need for courage in acting consistently with one's values and beliefs:

> I asked my executive if they believed we could succeed and if we had the right people in place. They all said no: each person believed they were doing a terrific job themselves but that none of their colleagues were. They had zero confidence in one another and in the team. I came to the conclusion that I had to make changes to my top team if we were going to succeed and in the end changed 60 per cent of that team. One of the guys I released went over my head and put pressure on me through Group. My boss in the US told me I couldn't let him go because of what he'd delivered, but he was cancerous and having a very negative effect on all he came into contact with. My boss said I had to reinstate him, but I refused and explained why. He chose to support me, but I knew that if the organization didn't deliver within two years it would be my time to leave. Fortunately it worked well, the new team gelled together very quickly and delivered a massive and sustained improvement in every metric from revenue, profit, market share, customer satisfaction and employee satisfaction. Working quickly on the dysfunctional team was essential to this.

Another storyteller spoke about leading an organization within an organization, his company having been acquired two years earlier:

> We've been doing very well the last two years. I've listened to the group mandate and made sure we're directionally correct even if we don't follow it to the letter. The risk is people begin to think we're some sort of breakaway republic. If the numbers falter they may hang me out to dry. That's a personal risk, but it's not my career – it's a job. If I was trying to be a corporate guy then I couldn't take risks. I used to work in private equity where your job is it; you sell the business, you lose your job. That's a good mindset to have at the senior

level. I'm not here to make them happy, but to do the right thing. It's a very liberating mental attitude.

Another storyteller spent time working closely with John Browne, CEO at the time of BP, a multinational energy company and one of the world's biggest organizations. In 1997 Browne delivered a now famous and sometimes maligned speech about climate change. In the speech he argued that organizations needed to take responsibility for the global environment and committed his organization to solutions to climate change: to managing its carbon dioxide emissions, to funding further research, to developing alternative fuels and to participating in the public dialogue. This was a courageous act. From our storyteller's perspective:

> He understood the aspirations of BP's employees in the context of society as a whole. This translated into the BP branding work, with the objective of creating a company that people would be proud of. The speech he made at Stanford was about companies needing to make a difference and he spoke about it in a public forum. He was courageous, with a value-based belief about wanting to improve the organization from within. He believed people wanted to work for a company that makes them proud, and to be part of making a difference. It was an ambitious message to embrace inside our organization and across the industry, but it was bold and courageous, and he was prepared to be attacked and criticized.

Moments of courage keep change programmes alive:

> The executive team thought it was all too hard. We had a number of sessions batting to and fro. Different functions came up with their own proposals without thinking they'd succeed. I took a proposal to them around setting up groups in the organization to have conversations around what might be possible. I put it up and got resistance. Then the engineering guy stood up and said 'Look. This is something we have to do. If we can't commit to this we might as well quit now.' He saw the possibility and stepped up to the plate. The room went quiet and everyone saw it at rational and emotional levels as if it was blindingly obvious. It all just tipped.

These moments of truth featured often in the stories I heard. The courage exhibited by the leaders of change appeared to be based on a deep level of self-awareness. This external practitioner spoke about an interaction with the CEO:

> I'd worked with him before. He ranted at me at one stage. I said to him, 'Do you believe if you shout at me you'll convince me? You demean yourself.'

I'm unshakeable. I believe in the goodness of people and that they deserve
to be respected. I'm grounded, centred and I know my limitations.

A senior manager spoke of the transformation of a not-for-profit organization from a small group of philanthropists to a sizeable organization. They
were challenged to introduce robust processes without losing their entrepreneurial spirit, a transformation that presented challenges to everyone.
The leader recognized he needed to publicly role-model a process of self-
examination and critique:

It helps that the CEO is brave. He commissioned a strategic review after he'd
already been around for quite a while. He opened himself up to the possibility
that his own behaviours could be changed. He role-modelled being relentlessly
self-critical, and always looking for a new way of doing things. Analysing
data with an open mind draws you to what needs to be done. The CEO put
himself at the heart of it and openly committed to do things differently, versus
defending himself because he was feeling criticized.

Change leaders therefore have to be prepared to take risks and to stand up
for what they believe. For the effective change leader this courage is based
on a strong sense of self.

Sincerity and authenticity

Authenticity is not the same thing as sincerity (Avolio and Gardner, 2005;
Trilling, 1972). Trilling defines sincerity as the congruence between what we
feel and what we say. So if I feel anxious at the prospect of change, and I
know I feel anxious, I am being sincere if I reveal to people that I'm feeling
anxious. If I tell everyone that I'm feeling super-confident and that I have no
concerns whatsoever as to the direction we're headed, then I'm not being
sincere. Authenticity is different. To be authentic is to behave in a way that is
congruent with an informed sense of self. To express oneself authentically is
difficult, not only because it requires being sincere but because it also involves
having an understanding of one's intended self, versus the self that others
wish for us. The sincere leader who speaks up for change with certainty and
conviction, yet feels suddenly unsure once the change begins to unfold that
this is what he actually wanted in the first place, is likely to change his tune
fairly frequently, or otherwise fail to present with a strong sense of conviction.
    The 2003 BBC television documentary 'Arsenic and Old Lace' provided
a stunning example of the difference between sincerity and authenticity. In

the programme, Gerry Robinson, a business consultant, is hired to advise the father–son owners of a lace-dyeing operation in the UK. Henry and Richard Chaplin buy the bankrupt business and endeavour to turn it round. They make a significant proportion of the workforce redundant and attempt to cajole and coerce the rest of the workforce into working harder. Instead of improving, performance at the factory deteriorates further. The workforce is demoralized and fearful and Robinson suggests that at the heart of the problem is the behaviour of the factory floor supervisor, Jeff, whose style is unrelentingly autocratic. Following some coaching by Robinson, Richard Chaplin calls a meeting on the factory floor where he delivers an impassioned speech in which he states his determination that the business will succeed and his belief in the workforce as the best workforce he has ever led. He announces the departure of Jeff and states that there will be no more redundancies. The speech is passionate, convincing and clearly sincere, and the workforce is visibly excited.

A week later Richard confesses he is no longer sure he has made the right decision, indeed wonders if it was the 'biggest blunder' of his career. He re-hires Jeff without telling the workforce why. Then a month later he announces a new wave of redundancies, almost half the workforce. Robinson is horrified, and it becomes obvious that though Richard is an earnest and sincere individual, he has little clarity in his own mind as to what kind of leader he wants to be, or what decisions to make.

The authentic leader knows himself well enough to be able to predict how he will respond to what lies ahead. His message is likely to be more consistent, more enduring and more energetic over time. This is important to understand, because it says authenticity isn't only a matter of sincerity or courage, but is a consequence of heightened self-awareness. The more open to learning you are, the more likely you are to become more authentic.

Meaning-making

Kegan (1994) provides a developmental lens on authenticity. He suggests humans go through up to five stages of development in the way that they interpret the world around them.

Young children inhabit the *first order,* in which things are as they seem. If a young child looks out from an aeroplane and sees tiny people walking around below, he believes the people are actually that small (Garvey Berger, 2006). There are no rules upon which to construct a different interpretation of the world. The world is magical place in which things may change from moment to moment.

From the age of about 7, children learn that objects stay the same no matter how big or small they may appear. They come to recognize the constancy of their own feelings and beliefs, and so come to realize this must be true of other people too. These older children become aware of the existence of rules, and begin to understand how other people function too, not through empathy but through deduction. People inhabiting this *second order* are sovereign in their own worlds, navigating the rules from a sense of what matters to them.

Not everyone develops further from this stage, but most people move to the *third order,* that of the 'socialized mind'. The socialized mind, according to Garvey Berger (2006), is a state in which people have developed the capacity to internalize the feelings and emotions of others: they are empathetic. Not only are they able to internalize the feelings and emotions of others, but they are largely guided by the feeling and emotions of 'significant' others. They can think abstractly and reflect on their actions, and can devote themselves to something greater than their own needs, but they have no strong internal reference point. These are people who make sense of the world by referencing what seems to be important to *other* people. Arguably we all find ourselves in this state from time to time, when our desire to please others and to be liked becomes of paramount importance. How hard it must be for a change leader inhabiting the third order to contemplate engaging in dialogue with a series of impassioned stakeholders whose views are likely to be conflicting. The dilemma for the change leader becomes how to please everyone.

Adults operating at the *fourth order* are also able to internalize the feelings and emotions of others, but in addition they have created a robust internal reference point. Those with a self-authored mind experience empathy and take the views of others into account when making decisions, but have their own self-guided, self-motivated, self-evaluative systems by which to make those decisions. The self-authored mind is thus better equipped to engage in dialogue without feeling overly stressed or anxious. Most of us, say Kegan and Garvey Berger, sit somewhere between the socialized mind and the self-authored mind in the way that we make meaning and come to decisions. This means that most of us feel some degree of discomfort at the thought of engaging in dialogue with people who are likely to express conflicting views.

We must be very careful in considering the nature of this fourth order. I have heard it expressed in terms of boundaries, such that the individual's sense of self in this state exists outside of his relationships with others. I don't think this is what the model is suggesting, for this would be akin to suggesting that the individual's sense of self is self-created rather than co-created. I prefer an interpretation that suggests that a person in this fourth order state is more aware of the co-creative process, rather than being subject to it.

A very few of us apparently see life through a self-transforming mind, the *fifth order*. These people see the structure of their inner system, which may be compared to other's systems. People in this state are more likely to see the similarities between people than they are to focus on what is different. This feels to me like a systemic perspective in which the co-creative nature of identity is fully appreciated and acknowledged.

Kegan's theory is about the way we make meaning and is a lovely metaphor for authenticity and thinking systemically. If authenticity is about behaving in ways that are consistent with a strong internalized sense of self, then it is also about being able to disentangle in the moment how we actually think or feel about something and what others are telling us we should be thinking or feeling. This requires high levels of self-awareness about those parts of me that are separate and distinct from those parts that are you, and the capacity to stand back and see myself and the system within which I'm operating from a distance.

In Kegan's language the journey through the five stages is about progressively moving what sits at the back of our mind to the front of our mind, or 'making object' that to which we were previously subject. It's described as a linear journey. I prefer to think of the five stages as five layers of an onion. The more layers I am able to see, the greater my capacity to switch perspectives in the moment.

Some of our leaders spoke about their personal experiences of change, and the importance of feeling grounded in the 'self-authorized' space. For example:

> I met with three people just today, three people all displaying strong emotions and me as the leader having to be neutral and helpful. I stayed earthed, plugged into what I believe in. I try to be the best that I can, but you can't compare yourself to someone else; we're all different. I hope that my legacy will be that I helped others to believe in themselves and to take ownership of that.

A CEO said of his journey home at the end of each day:

> You're not going to keep everyone happy all the time. When I'm driving home I think about the board, the staff, suppliers, clients and customers. If three of those five are happy, then that's good! If you try and keep all five happy all of the time, then you burn out.

Authenticity and feedback

If the journey toward greater authenticity is a journey toward heightened self-awareness and an enhanced capacity to differentiate oneself from others, how do we attain this state? Some texts emphasize the importance of being oneself. According to the definition of authenticity expressed here, seeking to be true to oneself isn't the same as being authentic; rather it is an expression of sincerity that often reveals the extent to which one is authentic or not.

To become more authentic requires enhanced self-awareness and seeking out feedback. Not everyone feels comfortable seeking out feedback however, so many organizations have introduced processes to make sure feedback is delivered. The most common organizational tools deployed for this purpose are the annual performance review and 360-degree assessments. While occasionally useful, these forms of feedback have significant limitations.

Performance reviews are often hurried and rushed, often timed to occur in a short period of time just before the end of the financial year. Feedback tends to be general and non-specific, often watered-down. Even when conducted well, because feedback is delivered only at specific times of the year there has usually elapsed a significant period of time between the behaviour and the feedback. The events referred to may be a blur for all concerned. 360-degree assessments are also imperfect instruments, the results subject to the extent to which evaluators can recall the past accurately, whether they generally like or dislike the person in question and how much they stereotype others (Eckert *et al*, 2010; Garavan *et al*, 1997; Van der Heijden and Nijhof, 2004). Raters are asked to evaluate people by numbers, but the numbers don't tell the story.

These tools also tend to refer to generic definitions of good leadership and are based on highly individualistic models. The individual may not be supported in accessing his own, authentic, model of leadership, nor in seeking to understand how the way he is being perceived is a function of the context in which he is operating, including the values and beliefs held by others, and the overarching identity of the organization in question.

To become more authentic requires an ongoing commitment to asking for feedback and a systemic perspective from which to interpret the feedback received. A genuine commitment to asking for feedback means being open to the idea we are different to other people, that others define us differently to the way we define ourselves, indeed that we may not be certain how we want to define ourselves. In a sense it requires being comfortable with not knowing who we are. A systemic perspective helps us to see how people's responses to requests for feedback reflect their own values and beliefs, and how those values and beliefs are shaped through interactions with others. To ask for feedback is to seek an understanding of the system and the identity we have assumed within it.

Seeking feedback is one means by which to explore one's authentic self. Chapters 16 and 17 consider more broadly how to cultivate greater authenticity from a more systemic perspective. Authenticity breeds authenticity (Kernis, 2003); in other words authenticity fosters more positive affective states in others. The authentic leader brings an enhanced capacity to listen, voice and reflect any dialogue in which he participates. Others will attempt to emulate the behaviour, thereby becoming more self-aware and authentic themselves. Authenticity is a team and an organizational phenomenon, not just an individual phenomenon, and the change leader who thinks more systemically or holistically will seek to create dialogic spaces in which people generally are likely to become more authentic.

KEY POINTS

- We are the story we tell ourselves. Some people hold a story and choose not to reflect upon it. They may speak with sincerity, but their version of the story is unlikely to be well-informed. To be ill-informed is to lack self-awareness, which is to lack authenticity.

- Every choice we make reveals something about ourselves and constitutes an opportunity to learn something new about ourselves. To reflect on our actions is to take the opportunity to become more self-aware and thereby more authentic.

- To become more authentic is to become increasingly confident in the veracity of the story we tell about ourselves in relation to others. From this confidence comes courage.

- Courage and purpose inspire us to seek feedback from others, which in turn helps us to become more self-aware, more authentic and more courageous.

- Authenticity is a journey and no one is 100-per-cent authentic.

Resistance to change

11

'**R**esistance to change' is a commonly used term in the change literature, usually implying a general sense of organizational inertia (Shaw, 1997). Traditional models of change privilege the perspective of the change leader and demonize the recipient of change. A senior executive, or group of executives, interpret the data at their disposal on the basis of their own experience and come up with a logic for change which they then communicate to the rest of the organization. Without the opportunity to engage in dialogue not everyone may immediately embrace the change. The instigators of change may interpret reluctance to embrace the suggested change as a general reluctance to change, a denial of what is evidently true, or even insubordination. A common response to such 'intransigence' is to keep repeating the message ('communicate, communicate, communicate') through various channels in the hope that repetition will engender compliance. Objections, or even just questions, may be interpreted as dissent and discouraged, sometimes with the explicit threat of disciplinary action or the implicit threat of curtailed career prospects.

Resistance to change and the emerging change model

Through the lens of the emerging change model (ECM), resistance to change looks different. Consider the employee of a manufacturer/retailer. Helen works in a senior role in a regional sales office/call-centre operation. She talks to customers, suppliers, immediate co-workers and other colleagues in her networks. She's committed to improving customer service and has been participating in a cross-functional project for the last 12 months, the purpose of which is to improve systems insofar as they impact on the organization's capacity to service customers effectively. The project hasn't been going well, which the members of the project team attribute to a lack of visible sponsorship and support. It's proved impossible to get the project on to the senior management agenda, and team members have struggled to find time to both do their jobs and commit wholeheartedly to the project.

Meanwhile, the senior executives have been reviewing the organization's strategy. They are presented with evidence that suggests that they're spending more than their competitors on inferior customer service. They decide they need to both improve customer service and reduce costs, and renew their focus on the systems project, which doesn't seem to be making much progress. To try and kick-start the systems project they remove the project manager and bring in someone from outside the organization who's led similar projects for a consulting firm. They also increase incentives for successful completion. The executives then ask a change manager to compose an e-mail to explain the changes, and ask HR to implement the new incentives plan. They also tell the new project manager to travel out to the customer service centre to explain the changes in person at a town-hall meeting.

Helen receives the e-mail the day before the town hall meeting. It spells out the organization's determination to improve customer service through more efficient process and less staff. The rationale doesn't make sense. By reducing costs now, customer service will inevitably deteriorate. How can the team improve service with less resource? How will the project team deliver when she and the other team members will now have to do more work covering for staff that won't be replaced? And why has the project manager been replaced by an outsider, given that he has spent the last twelve months building strong relationships across the organization? She talks to her colleagues who have the same questions as she does. Between them they come up with some key questions to ask the project manager at the town hall.

The project manager, meanwhile, is keen and enthusiastic. He delivered a similar project at another organization the year before. It started slowly, but once he replaced a few key personnel the team really got into its stride and delivered results ahead of time. He arrives ten minutes before he's due to speak and proceeds to the meeting room. He notices that people seem unenthused, and so begins his talk in deliberately upbeat tempo, telling the team about his earlier successes, how he sees the challenges based on what he's been told by senior management, and how sure he is that the team will be successful. Once he's finished he asks for questions. Helen puts up her hand and asks him how the project can be successful when the team is already under-resourced even before the new round of cost cutting. The project manager grits his teeth and repeats what he's already said; about the success he's had in previous projects, the support he's been promised by head office, and his belief in the power of a positive attitude. Someone else puts up their hand and repeats a version of Helen's question. The project manager provides much the same answer as he did the first time before calling an end to the meeting and heading back to head office where he complains to the senior executives about the team's resistance to change and his conviction that he will have to make significant changes to personnel.

From the perspective of the emerging change model there is more than one form of 'resistance' going on here. First, the senior executives have formed a view based on their own perspective of events and an external view – the consultant's report. They don't appear to have solicited the views or perspectives of the members of the project team, or indeed anyone in the regional office. It seems likely, on the basis of events thus far, that they will support the project manager and agree with his recommendations. They don't appear disposed to explore the views of Helen and her colleagues; they are resisting that perspective and in effect refusing to hear it.

The project manager has arrived with a predetermined view of what the issues are likely to be. He arrived at the town hall with an intention to tell others about that view and an expectation that others would find it compelling. Faced with a lack of enthusiasm, he immediately interpreted that behaviour as reflecting a general unwillingness to embrace change. He took the questions as read and made no attempt to understand what might be underlying the views as expressed. In effect he is resisting the idea that his perspective of events may not be fully informed.

Helen and her colleagues are frustrated because no one seems interested in what they have to say. That said, at the town hall they too appeared unwilling to explore the project manager's perspective. After Helen asked her question, someone else asked the same question. No one asked the project manager about his previous experience, or of the outcome of the dialogue he had with the senior executives.

Every interaction in the scenario is monologic. There is no dialogue between the regional operation and the project manager, or between the regional operation and the senior executives. It is quite likely there has been little dialogue between the project manager and the senior executives either; the executives have explained the situation as they see it and the project manager has told them what he thinks needs to happen based on his experiences elsewhere.

In short, the key stakeholders all appear to be resisting each other's perspectives, but because the senior executives and the project manager hold the positional power, the official story is likely to feature 'resistance to change' only on the part of the regional office. Each of the stakeholders is well-intentioned, indeed all the stakeholders appear to share a common desire to improve customer service and implement a new system. But at this stage of the story it appears unlikely that will happen.

Van Dijk and van Dick (2009) suggest that most management literature privileges the perspective of the change leader. 'Resistance' has come to mean anything workers do that management doesn't want them to do and the change leader is considered to be 'on the side of the angels' while the reluctant masses are characterized as 'mulish and obstinate' (Thomas and Hardy, 2011).

Sources of resistance

One of our storytellers said: 'People don't resist undertaking change – they do resist having change done to them.' Another said: 'People who are pushed, push back.'

Another talked about the use of the word 'change' as having come to mean change for the sake of change, a time-consuming set of activities that leads to no discernible improvement but carries with it the threat of loss of control, of status, or even of a job:

> Change threatens people, so don't run a 'change' programme, run a programme of what you're going to do. 'Change' is an unhelpful label; it can freeze an organization. People get scared, or start digging their heels in and making conditions. Much better is to say what it is you want to achieve. For example, 'Let's improve engagement with our customers so that they look to us for advice and increase their level of business with us. We will put together a team of our best people to work out how we do that.' People love it and want to jump on it. If you come in saying you want to do a change programme which is non-specific, it just creates uncertainty and fear.

Van Dijk and van Dick (2009) list various sources of resistance to change including diminished job security, being required to do more work for less money, a fear that the changes will make no difference, and a threat to identity. We've already come across examples in Chapter 8 of people who feared their identity would be compromised by a proposed change. This CEO tells a similar story of an individual whose identity came under threat by a proposed change:

> It's been a tough slog. I still have a member of my staff who constantly talks about 'how we are' when it's actually 'how we were'. It's not resistance; it's what he believes in and is comfortable with.

Reissner (2010) compares identity to a rock in the middle of a storm; a safe place to cling to when nothing else makes much sense. To release one's grip on the rock too early is to abdicate responsibility for one's own identity, to trust in others that we will feel at ease behaving in a way that is at odds with the story we currently tell about ourselves. Most people try hard not to let go of the rock, but to make sense of the 'change' by talking it through with others they trust. We may be open to changes to our identity but that doesn't mean we are prepared to allow others to rewrite the story for us in whatever way they please. A significant change initiative often constitutes an attempt to redefine identities. From this perspective 'resistance to change' means a resistance to having someone else redefine our identity for us. If the change leader's story doesn't make sense in terms of the stories we tell about ourselves and others, and/or the new story is asking us to adopt new identities that don't feel safe, we are likely to question it. Responding to such questions by constantly repeating the same message over and over is unlikely to do much good.

So-called 'resistance to change' is based in part upon the fact that we all see things differently. The first step in addressing such 'resistance' is to consider the notion that resistance is often motivated by the best of intentions (Piderit, 2000).

Resistance as resource

This storyteller sought to change the business model of her organization, making it more customer-responsive and lower cost. This involved partnering with an overseas service provider:

> Internally people said that no one likes talking to overseas call centres, but the most recent research says that the quality of the best overseas call centres is very high. Nevertheless, the resistance made the quality better. We recognized we had to make sure there was no way we were perceived to be compromising service for the sake of cutting cost. We worked with our partners to make sure we brought in only the highest quality people. We took the unknown out of the equation and got everyone talking about it continually. We asked people, 'Tell us what you're worried about,' and listened to the answers. Not everything went well and what we did about it was important. For example, we had a lot of input into selection and training, and we asked for a few people to be removed early who we didn't feel were good enough on the phones.

An external practitioner had this to say:

> You're supposed to get resistance if it's a change. If it's not there then you need to expend a lot of energy trying to find it – it means people haven't delved deep enough. If people sign off on the business case for change too easily it means the business case doesn't spell out clearly enough what will happen to different parts of the business. It requires dialogue, otherwise you'll encounter resistance later on down the track.

McClellan (2011) suggests that one of the reasons change efforts are unsuccessful is because the monologic approach to communication results in the suppression of conflicting meanings. To suppress the expression of different points of view is to perpetuate the fragmentation of the collective perspective. Ford *et al* (2008) suggest reframing resistance to change. Instead of thinking of resistance as an unwelcome obstacle, they see it as a way of making sure the dialogue takes place. If people are unsure what a change means, they will carry on talking about it until they succeed in making sense of it. Resistance in this sense is much better than indifference, since resistance implies a need to 'make sense' and therefore a desire to engage in dialogue. In a similar vein, Thomas and Hardy (2011) talk about celebrating resistance, leveraging resistance to shift people's attention to the subject in question, thereby stimulating a dialogue from which new insights and understanding will emerge. Resistance helps stimulate dialogue.

Reciprocal resistance

As discussed, many change narratives frame change only from the perspective of the change leader. From this standpoint change leaders are doing the 'right thing' while change recipients focus on 'screwing up' the change (Ford and Ford, 2010). Change leaders are portrayed as frustrated victims of irrational and dysfunctional organizations. In this case 'resister' is a label applied by one group to another group who don't agree with their point of view. Resistance is 'out there' and not 'in here'. If we stand outside of the hierarchical perspective then it becomes apparent that anyone can label anyone else as being resistant to change, since it basically seems to mean not listening.

This is not a frame likely to be embraced by those change leaders whose subscription to the sanctity of positional power is supported by the multitude of books and articles out there in the change world that frame 'resistance to change' within a hierarchical framework. To consider the possibility that one's own perspective may be incomplete, to cede the possibility of a different vision of the future, and to consider that one might not be willing to listen, requires a degree of self-awareness and reflection. This loops us back to Chapters 5 and 10 in which we discussed the critical role of reflection in learning and the development of authenticity. To consider oneself as the blocker of change may require an extraordinary paradigm shift on the part of a leader. This senior executive describes coming to terms with his own need to change. He had been hired by a public service organization to implement a change agenda:

> At first I came unstuck. I assumed everyone was on the same page as the CEO. In the first year I ended up having several fights until I realized that the CEO didn't want to command his direct reports. He worked on the basis of individual relationships and was hoping everyone walked away with the same message. In fact they walked away with different messages. I didn't understand the environment, people's objectives, their capabilities or capacities. I thought I was doing the right thing, building relationships with stakeholders but I was missing things. Coming from the private sector it took me a while to realize that the most important agenda for many people was to protect their pension. The organizational mission was second or third priority. I had to challenge myself. I asked myself what I believed in. Was I being egotistical? It took the air out of my tyres when I realized there was a bit of ego. I was approaching relationships assuming we'd have a battle, versus putting strategies in place to create productive relationships. I had got hung up on my personal values and had become resentful of the CEO and the organization. I recognized the need to step up to the balcony and suck in some air. I realized no one was out to get me personally and yet it was my natural instinct to go into defence mode. I had misread the environment but was also in the dark with myself. That was my reflection, and after that I instituted some feedback loops.

It's not easy being a change leader espousing a change that will significantly impact people's lives, that may result in people being asked to move home or being made redundant. The change leader may feel uncertain and unclear, worried what questions and challenges may arise. This is a threatening scenario for the change leader, whose own identity is under threat. If I aspire to be a strong unwavering leader, resolute and confident, what will it mean if I fail to answer people's questions to their satisfaction? What will it mean if I look nervous? If the identity I aspire to is the wise insightful leader, what does it mean if people disagree with my vision for the future? Just as the identities of the recipients of change can slow change down, so can the identities of the change leaders.

People and buses

In Chapter 8 I discussed identity and the need to give people time to come to terms with the meaning of change with reference to their identities. Frustration with 'resistance to change' is often a reflection of a frustration that people aren't agreeing quickly enough with the proposed change. This plays into the idea of organizational inertia. For those who approach change solely from a logical perspective, it must be frustrating when things inexplicably take longer to implement than they would if people would simply do as they were told and doff their hat to reason and logic.

Does this need for time to question and process prove that people are by nature resistant? This CEO found his efforts thwarted from all sides, including the board:

> In legacy organizations you find a brick wall of resistance which manifests itself in belligerence and the rejection of outsiders: 'You're new to this industry – what do you know?' There is always a way to resist and so you find yourself neutered, in a zone of irrelevance; advanced management antibody syndrome, repelling the invader army. Opinions are based on rumours rather than a rational, logical business case. To manage this degree of stupidity requires the patience of Job.

This leader spoke specifically about resistance and the need for time:

> I think you have to have a lot of tolerance for defensive behaviours. People want to understand, and we created opportunities for debate and discussion. Some people move on; often for career advancement, sometimes because people don't like the direction. We were very good at supporting people when they wanted to leave. We worked hard to ensure people left feeling good about the organization. That's different to the place I worked before, where those who said they were going were dead people walking. Reducing the personal downside reduces barriers to change.

Twenty-eight per cent of storytellers spoke about the need to ask people to leave an organization, but there emerged two quite different perspectives. Consider this storyteller's account of an imposed change, forced through an organization that was under threat of being closed down by the regulator:

> Post GFC, governments all over the world were imposing stricter controls and regulations. We had no wriggle room and demanded compliance. One leader effectively fired someone who breached the car parking rules three times. It became part of the story: a good trader got fired for parking wrongly.

Contrast that to this story:

> Not everyone came on the journey. Two people left within six months. It
> was a combination of all the change taking place in the organization and
> the difficulties they experienced in transitioning to where the rest of the
> team wanted to go. We helped them transition successfully. One experienced
> executive said, 'I'm not up for this.' It was disappointing but I respected it. It
> was a fork in the road for him and you need to ensure people feel they can
> make the right choice. I lost some experience and gained some fresh blood.

Traditional approaches to change encourage practitioners to label people
quickly as either being 'on the bus' or 'off the bus'. This implies an expectation that people must quickly declare their allegiance to the change agenda.
If this is the prevailing culture then most people will declare themselves 'on
the bus' regardless of their actual commitment. In these kinds of organizations change may be hard to implement, since commitment and energy
levels are likely to be low. In contrast, I heard lots of stories in this study
where people were asked to leave, but only after having the opportunity to
engage in dialogue, to exchange perspectives with others in the organization
and to come to their own conclusion that the new organizational identity
was no longer in synch with their own needs and wants. People are likely
to feel more empowered in the second scenario. They are more likely to feel
listened to. They may well look back and consider the experience as a positive experience in which they learnt new things about themselves relative to
others.

Effective change agency

This chapter pulled together strands from previous chapters about the nature
of 'resistance to change'. Such resistance is often framed as the belligerence
and contrariness of those firmly committed to the status quo. The change
leader responds to this resistance by issuing the same message time and time
again until the message can no longer be ignored, smashing through the
thick shell of resistance with a club of indisputable logic, or else by threatening punitive measures to those who refuse to vacate their shells willingly.

The stories I heard suggested that such approaches are unlikely to succeed. The successful change leader is more likely to regard 'resistance' as a
desire to engage in dialogue, and to make time for dialogue. The successful
change leader recognizes that resistance is a process that requires time for
people to make meaning. Often people emerge from this meaning-making

process newly enthused and aligned. Sometimes people emerge believing that their sense of who they are and what the organization needs to be doesn't fit with the proposed change. Where this is the case, sadly, the best thing for individual and organization may be to go their separate ways. Resistance is a way into this dialogue. Without the dialogue people will feel unheard and disrespected. As one of our storytellers, an ex-CEO, said: 'You can't not have resistance. It's not always resistance anyway. You must always be listening and testing.'

KEY POINTS

- 'Resistance to change' is a term often used by change leaders to describe the intransigence of people further down the organization.

- The proponents of change are often as 'resistant' as the recipients of change, as demonstrated by their unwillingness to consider other perspectives.

- Resistance is different to indifference. Resistance often implies passionate good intentions and a desire to engage in dialogue. To decline the invitation to engage in dialogue may be to decline the possibility of effective change.

Systemic thinking

12

In Chapter 5 we considered reflection. I adopted Stacey's (2012) definition of reflection as abstraction, standing away from events and thinking about the meaning of those events. I also wrote about some of the busy people I come across in organizations who seem to be struggling to make time to stand back and adopt a broader perspective. I related the story of a coachee who pointed at an empty coffee mug and compared the view from the bottom of the mug with the view from the rim. His goal was to spend more time on the rim of the mug. What we didn't talk about, however, was what the view might look like from the edge of the room, or from the street outside, or from the top of a tall building. In this chapter we'll consider different levels of reflection and how that links to the idea of systemic thinking. First let's be clear what we mean by 'systemic'.

Systematic and systemic, complicated and complex

Sammut-Bonnici and Wensley (2002) differentiate between complicated and complex systems. Complicated systems may be difficult to understand, but can be broken down into their constituent parts with enough time and effort. Complex systems can never be fully understood or modelled because there are too many variables at play, connected to each other through a multitude of changing relationships leading to unpredictable outcomes. Litchenstein (1996) suggests that many senior executives fail to implement change or strategies successfully because they are trained to solve complicated problems rather than complex ones, and have been successful in the past because of their outstanding intellectual ability.

Clutterbuck and Megginson (2005) distinguish between 'systematic' and 'systemic'. Adopting a systematic approach is to adopt an orderly and linear approach. A systematic approach in the change context is often top-down and linear with an emphasis on great planning, an approach that makes sense if we view the world as complicated. A systemic approach is based on a belief that the world is complex, not merely complicated. The systemic approach also encourages us to stand back and see the bigger picture, but not in service of trying to understand everything for there are too many variables at play for this to be a useful goal. The danger of the systematic approach is that we stop being curious once we think we have grasped the nature of the whole. The systemic approach is to see how an over-emphasis on planning can be to blind oneself to the complexity of one's surroundings and the need to review one's actions and make adjustments continuously as one goes along.

In this book we are not using the term 'systemic thinking' to mean 'systematic thinking' or to advocate that the change leader needs to try and understand each and every aspect of his environments and the links between those aspects. Here we use systemic thinking to mean the practice of continually stepping back and stepping forth, engaging in the system as a player then assessing the impact of our actions before engaging once more as a player; or to mean stepping forth and back at the same time, to be holding multiple perspectives simultaneously, reflecting upon our actions in the moment.

The approach to change implied by the emerging change model is one in which the environment is always changing in ways that are often unpredictable and surprising. While we can attempt to use models to represent the environment, the use of models should not engender a false sense of assurance that the alluringly simple perspective thus created is in any sense 'true'. While models used well are useful, the more important task is to be continually leveraging multiple perspectives in service of navigating a successful journey through unpredictable waters, choppy and changeable. Models may be used to represent the simple and the complicated, but can never represent the whole picture of that which is complex (Sargent and McGrath, 2011).

The view from the balconies

The 'view from the balcony' metaphor is a popular one. According to the metaphor we may choose to locate ourselves on the dance-floor, in which case our perspective is limited to the action immediately surrounding us, or else we can climb to the balcony where we can see what everyone is doing. This has the same meaning as the coffee cup metaphor described earlier. There are lots of similar metaphors in the English language, for example the difference between seeing the wood and the trees, being able to see the bigger picture, etc.

Thinking about the difference between systematic thinking and systemic thinking, there is a risk that these metaphors may encourage us to think

FIGURE 12.1 Views from the balconies

systematically rather than systemically. The balcony metaphor appears to imply that if we stand back and reflect from a loftier vantage point then we will see the world in its entirety. We will see all the people dancing and be able to work out how events in one corner of the room lead to events in another corner. Again, taken literally, the metaphor implies there are only two vantage points, the view from within the event and the view from outside the event.

A more complete metaphor may be to consider the view from the balconies (plural). Figure 12.1 shows a number of balconies with different vantage points. Consider the following example.

John is annoyed with Sarah, who works for him. He's annoyed because she didn't complete a piece of work he had been waiting on for several days even though she assured him it would get done. He takes a deep breath and in his mind ascends to the balcony where he can see an angry version of himself trying to stay calm while Sarah regards him anxiously, expecting him to remonstrate with her. From the balcony he can see all the other people asking Sarah for help, and sees how she is struggling to accommodate all these different demands. He no longer feels annoyed and determines to help her, by suggesting she attend a time management course, for example. In Figure 12.1, let's call this balcony A.

Had John climbed to balcony B instead of A then he would have had a different vantage point. The events were the same, but from balcony B John sees different aspects of what's happening on the dance floor. He sees others asking for help, and sees her agreeing but then failing to either meet her commitments or let others know in advance she can't deliver. He feels less sympathetic of Sarah's plight and is more focused on wanting her (and everyone else who works for him) to be more accountable. From this vantage point John believes Sarah should have recognized her inability to deal with multiple requests and should have addressed it sooner, raising it with him if necessary. He resolves to speak to her about the importance of accountability and to coach her accordingly.

From balcony C the world looks different again. From this higher vantage point John notices how Sarah isn't the only one struggling with accountability. He sees everyone on his team running around struggling to get things done, unclear as to who's agreed to do what. There is simply too much to do and most people have become fixated solely on their own deliverables. John feels guilty and decides to get the team together to work out how to prioritize better and how to work more effectively as a team.

From balcony D John notices how his behaviour as the leader of the team, particularly his focus on accountability, is a consequence of his relationship with his line manager, Tracey. Tracey seems to have high expectations of him. She talks about the need for him to build a strong team and the need to stay focused on strategy, yet she keeps giving him more and more work to do. He sees some of his peers struggling but others managing, and suspects he's being tested somehow. He recognizes that he is struggling in his relationship with Tracey and recognizes how his own assumptions and beliefs may be playing out in that relationship such that he finds it difficult to challenge her.

From balcony E John sees Tracey interacting with her peers and sees how the interaction of those different personalities is playing out with their teams and the interactions between those teams. Standing this high up John not only has a much better understanding of who he is being as a leader and how this is playing out in all the different relationships he has with people at work, but all sorts of other possibilities arise for him as to how he can be more effective in his relationships with Sarah, his team, Tracey, Tracey's boss and various other people in different teams around the organization.

There are other balconies we could go to with John, different levels of reflection. Some of these reflective perspectives will prove more useful than others in plotting an effective intervention in the 'system'. The balconies metaphor is a good depiction of the reflective process as defined by van de Ven and Sun (2011), a process by which we continually revisit the mental models we deploy to help us best understand what may be happening.

Over-privileging and under-communicating a balcony perspective

From a balcony, on a clear and cloudless evening, everything looks sharp and clear. While the view may include many features, there appears a natural order to the world; everything fits together and makes sense. What can't be seen in detail appears too small to worry about. What can't be seen from this particular balcony appears unimportant. It's at this point that the change leader risks over-privileging the view from a particular balcony, forgetting the importance of dialogue and the value of exploring the view from other vantage points. Dialogue becomes monologue and the change leader forgets to listen.

Equally, the change leader may forget to voice the view from the balcony, assuming others share the same perspective. This local CEO was startled to discover one day that he was the only one who understood the global organization's strategy:

> I found out by accident that no one on the top team could articulate our value
> proposition. We were at a quarterly leadership meeting with 70 leaders and

managers invited. The purpose of the meeting was to share what was going on. A facilitator joined us for a half-day session as part of the two days. In his session he asked the room, 'What are your company's objectives? What do you stand for? Who's your customer?' No one could answer. The more times he asked the question the worse the answers. People mumbled incoherent bits of sentences from the annual report that made absolutely no sense and it was clear no one understood or could articulate what we stood for. I couldn't believe it; there was so much material around, how could our leaders not have read, understood and be able to articulate it with passion? I brooded until the afternoon of the second day when I told them what I thought. They were the leaders of the company, how could they expect anyone to follow if they did not know where they were going? I was furious! People had lost their way and their focus. We'd gone from being a company where everyone knew who we were, before the dotcom crash, to being beaten, and our leaders were sitting there and taking it. How did it happen, with some of the smartest go-getters in the country? To my surprise the leaders responded incredibly well to my berating them. We put in place an education programme for every single person in the company to learn who we were. It was great to see people pick this up and articulate it in their own words and to see how much more confident they became in the market, and we certainly saw the impact in our results.

When the change leader steps up to a balcony, he must remind himself to come back down again, to hear what others are seeing from their more proximate standpoints, and to explain to others what he can see over the horizon.

The emerging change model and systems thinking

The traditional model of change is based on the premise that the world is simple enough to understand through the collection of data, the logical analysis of which will deliver a rationally indisputable course of action. The world is a pretty stable place, but every now and again things happen that call for a response. The role of the change leader in this scenario is to ensure the analytical process is properly conducted so that the change is understood and an appropriate response determined. A call for action should then be issued to which the whole organization is duty bound to respond. Those who fail to respond must be constantly reminded until they oblige, or sacrificed in full view of others in an attempt to stir them from their inertia.

The emerging change model is based on a view of the world that says the world is too complex to hope to be able to analyse from a single vantage point, no matter how elevated that perspective. Any attempt to discern an objectively indisputable course of action is unlikely to succeed, for complexity implies a myriad of different vistas, interpretations and hypotheses as to the best course of action to take. Organizations are full of people, people with different values and beliefs as to what constitutes the most desirable vision, and these people are all located within an ever-shifting web of relationships.

The task of the change leader includes engaging with people, engaging in dialogue, seeking to understand where other people are coming from and the nature of their relationship with any given change. It includes watching to see who is talking to who and where; what these groups of people are talking about and the sense they are making of the organization and its environment as it continues to change. It means working out how most effectively to engage in that meaning-making process, when to say what to who and when. It entails being aware of organizational dynamics and watching for the influence of power on the way that people relate to each other and make meaning together.

This approach to change clearly requires of the effective change leader the capacity to extract himself from the immediacy of day-to-day interactions, the anxieties and frustrations of managing ambiguity, and to continually take stock of what's just happened and what to do next. In the words of Clutterbuck and Megginson (2005), change is a process that requires 'humility, patience, courage, and open-minded experimentation'. In the words of one of our storytellers:

> You can't script a change. The real success is around assessing where you are at any given time and assessing what's needed at that time and getting people at that moment to do those things.

KEY POINTS

- The term 'systems thinking' may be used to describe two quite different philosophies. 'Systematic' thinking implies an orderly and linear approach. 'Systemic' thinking, as defined here, assumes the world is too complex to regard systematically.

- We can also differentiate between complicated systems and complex systems. Complicated systems can be broken down into their constituent parts with enough time and effort. Complex systems can never be fully understood or modelled.

- To think systemically means continually stepping back and forth, engaging in the system as a player then stepping back to assess the impact of our actions, before engaging once more as a player.

- Systemic thinking is process without parameters. Models and tools may help us to view the system from a particular perspective, but there are many different models and an infinite number of perspectives from which to view the system.

- Many of us get so sucked into doing that we fail to make the time to regard the world systemically; to explore our surroundings with fresh eyes, to engage in dialogue with people with different perspectives, and to continually review what we are doing, how and why.

PART FIVE
Application

Case study: The emerging change model in practice

13

In this chapter I will attempt to demonstrate how the emerging change model may prove useful in practice. In doing so I will illustrate how the model is best used, not as a linear process but as a framework for reflection and representation of how change happens anyway.

This is the story of a change programme that has been unfolding alongside the writing of this book. I've deliberately chosen an example of a programme initiated by a function outside the executive, first, because many change initiatives are not initiated by the executive and second, because many change advocates find it difficult to get the senior executive to sponsor their projects. Change advocates often find it difficult to access the senior executive, or else find the executive unwilling to proactively advocate their programme as requested.

I've also deliberately chosen a relatively simple programme in a medium-sized organization and decided to tell only part of the story. To attempt to tell the whole story of the bigger change effort would be a topic of a book in itself. My objective is to tell a simple story of a complex change effort so as to illustrate aspects of using the ECM in practice.

The organization concerned is a medium-sized manufacturer/distributor/retailer, with a factory in Australia and retail operations in Australia, China, the United States and Europe. The company was founded as a privately owned company, and was acquired a few years ago by a company listed on an Asian stock exchange.

The change programme

In the beginning

At our first meeting the OD manager explained that the company had recently conducted a survey suggesting that many people didn't feel highly engaged. The company later started analysing staff turnover numbers, data that appeared to support this conclusion. The company was growing fast, across different territories, and the CEO had recently expressed concerns about the lack of candidates ready to step up into executive team roles. The OD manager proposed contracting a small team of executive coaches to work with potential successors to the executive team, a suggestion the CEO agreed to on the basis of his own positive experience of having been coached.

The employee engagement survey highlighted a general lack of satisfaction with opportunities to develop. To address this, the OD manager decided to advocate the value of a 'coaching culture' in which coaching would sit at the heart of how people interacted with each other, in service of increasing staff engagement, people development and performance. She wasn't sure, she said, where the executive team sat on the matter. She knew that the CEO valued an entrepreneurial culture free of excessive process or bureaucracy, but beyond that there had been little dialogue as to what the culture should look like. In practice people were very busy, driven by high growth expectations to get things done, focused on short-term deliverables.

The purpose of the emerging change model is to help us reflect on what we've experienced, enabling us to step back and see change from a broader perspective. We can frame the first dialogue between us and the OD manager with reference to the ECM model (see Figure 13.1). Two weeks later we spoke to the CEO.

A dialogue with the CEO

The CEO began by reiterating what we had heard about the business strategy, emphasizing how quickly the business was growing and the need to develop the capacity of the organization accordingly. When we asked him what the purpose of deploying executive coaches in the business was, he quickly stated the need to accelerate the development of potential successors to the members of his management team. When we asked him what the purpose of rolling out coaching skills programmes was, he admitted to being uncertain. When the OD manager explained her rationale for the training he agreed and sanctioned the work to go ahead. He also agreed to give the OD manager some time at a senior executive meeting to explain the purpose of the programme and discuss how the senior executive team could support it. On the face of it this was a successful meeting, but on reflection we realized the extent to which we had become distracted and allowed this to impact on our listening (see Figure 13.2).

FIGURE 13.1 Our first dialogue with the OD manager

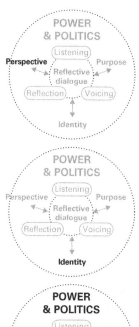

The OD manager had a personal perspective on some of the issues related to the desired culture change, but a limited understanding of other's views.

She brought an identity to the dialogue consistent with having recently attained a Master's degree in coaching. She saw an aspect of her role as being to advocate and role-model coaching behaviours.

She recognized that the CEO tended to work independently of his executive team, acting as a gateway to the agenda and choosing to manage some issues on behalf of the executive team.

She told us that the organization was quite siloed, with tensions existing between different functions and geographies. Few forums existed in the organization for reflective dialogue.

She recognized that the CEO was not yet aligned with the purpose of the work she was proposing. She subsequently set up a meeting with him to discuss what that purpose might be.

FIGURE 13.2 Our first dialogue with the CEO

We heard the CEO speak emphatically about the need to develop successors to his team, but didn't fully explore his rationale. Instead we probably assumed we understood what he was talking about based on our own view on the importance of succession planning.

We heard the CEO express doubts as to the purpose of rolling our coaching skills programmes, but didn't probe deeply enough to help him frame what that purpose might be.

Though the CEO talked about his desire to further encourage the building of an 'entrepreneurial' culture, we didn't probe deeply enough to understand what that meant. Nor did we explore some of the tensions he may have been experiencing given his belief in a culture free of process and bureaucracy. This entrepreneurship seemed to be part of his identity as a leader.

In short, despite our best intentions, we didn't do a great job in facilitating an effective dialogue. We were overly focused on voicing our own enthusiasm for the coaching programme and allowed that enthusiasm to get in the way of our listening and reflection in-the-moment.

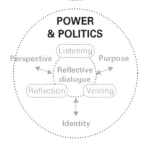

One of the factors that may have got in the way of our listening was an awareness of an imbalance in power. We found ourselves very much attuned to his ability to sanction or disapprove our proposals. At the same time the CEO may have contributed to this outcome by sanctioning the programme without further challenging its value. To what extent were these dynamics showing up elsewhere in the organization?

The limited extent to which we engaged in effective dialogue may explain why the OD manager subsequently found it difficult to get access to one of the quarterly senior executive team meetings. Despite finding it hard to meaningfully engage the CEO and executive team in a conversation about purpose, the OD manager pushed on, personally delivering programmes in each market around the globe. Several members of the executive team were assigned coaches, as were those identified as having long-term potential to develop into an executive role.

The OD manager also agreed to a programme of ongoing evaluation, seeking to understand how the 'coaching culture' was developing over time. She identified 25 people across the organization, people from different levels, functions and territories, including the CEO and the executive team. We agreed that I would interview everyone on the list at six-month intervals. The interviews would be treated as confidential and I would report back general themes and trends to the organization.

Listening to the organization

Before coaching and coaching skills training started I telephoned the 25 people and spoke to each of them for up to half an hour. I asked a series of questions seeking to understand how coaching was perceived in the organization, the purpose of coaching and how coaching related to the strategic goals of the business.

Talking to people I found apparent alignment around the purpose of coaching. This alignment, however, behind the fact that people were using the word 'coaching' to mean very different things. This actual lack of alignment was unlikely to change without new forums for dialogue, since the organization felt quite siloed, mirroring the ways in which the executive themselves appeared to communicate (Figure 13.3).

The CEO and HR director were keen to hear the outcome of the interviews. They listened to the findings and decided again that the OD manager should attend a senior executive meeting to facilitate a dialogue, the primary objective of which would be to come up with a shared definition of 'coaching', and how to support the coaching programme as it continued to roll out.

Programme rollout

Twelve people in the organization started their coaching assignments and coaching skills workshops were rolled out all over the business below the senior executive team level. The OD manager suggested putting the senior

FIGURE 13.3 Listening to the organization

Different people were using the word 'coaching' to mean different things. Some referred to any kind of developmental activity, including training. Others said coaching was about telling people what they needed to do. Only a small number of people defined coaching as an activity that started with listening. One person felt deflated at the extent to which she was being micromanaged. She was being coached though, she said, because coaching included managers telling their staff how to do their job.

On the face of it there appeared to be significant alignment onthe purpose of coaching. People believed that coaching was about developing people, and that the company needed to develop people to meet its challenging business growth targets. However, because people were using the word 'coaching' to mean different things, in practice there was no clear picture as to what this coaching culture would look like.

It became clear during the interviews just how busy people were all over the business. Some people were working extremely long hours and managers generally appeared to see themselves as 'expert doers', an identity likely to act as a barrier to spending time on people development.

There appeared to be little dialogue going on around the organization, with silos having formed and relationships between the centre and the regions often feeling strained. People talked about their discomfort in giving feedback and their unhappiness at not being listened to, evidence of a monologic culture in which people focused on telling others what they needed to do to in order to meet what they understood to be the company's overall goals.

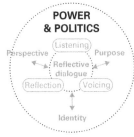

The silos appeared to reflect the extent to which members of the executive team focused primarily on the workings of their own teams. They came together once a quarter, and the primary conduit between team leaders appeared \to be the CEO himself, who had weekly calls with most of his direct reports individually. Evidence of the role of the CEO emerged when I asked people who was sponsoring the coaching work. Most people named the CEO and relatively few named the senior executive team.

executive team through a shortened version of the programme, but once more it proved difficult to persuade the CEO this was important enough to merit the executive's time.

Anecdotal evidence suggested that coaching skills training was effective. The programme was experiential and evidence-based, and class sizes were restricted to no more than 10 people to allow for plenty of dialogue and reflection. The OD manager followed up workshops with regular telecons, providing further opportunity for people to engage in dialogue after the programme finished.

Six months later I listened again to 23 of the original 25 people (two had left the organization). By this time 18 of the 23 had either been coached or attended a coaching skills workshop. I found some shifts in perspectives and the emergence of 'coalitions'.

Those people who attended the coaching skills workshops now spoke about coaching in similar terms, with a new emphasis on empowerment and helping people work out what to do for themselves. Those who hadn't attended the workshops, including people who had been coached, were more likely to talk about coaching-as-telling or coaching-as-training. The emergence of this new coalition led to an explicit fragmentation of purpose, and some shifts in identity. The workshops themselves had become a forum for dialogue in which people were exploring a new collective identity together, and in which they began to express some impatience with those holding positional power (Figure 13.4).

Change!

Around this time the HR director moved into a new role, leaving a contractor to fill the HR role on an acting basis. Shortly after that the OD manager resigned, and then a few weeks later the CEO resigned as well. Christmas was a busy time and not much happened in the coaching space over the next six months. The coaching skills workshops all finished, and the OD manager wasn't around to support people in their learning, pending a new appointment.

Managers throughout continued to be coached, and it became clear that some coaching assignments were working better than others. Consistent with a more monologic definition of coaching, some people were approaching it expecting to receive specific guidance as to how they should perform their roles more effectively. The HR director spoke to people behind the scenes to help manage their expectations as to what they could hope to gain from coaching.

In April of the next year I spoke to 21 of the original 25 people, another two people having departed. I also interviewed the outgoing CEO, the new CEO and the new HR Director.

FIGURE 13.4 Listening to the organization again

Those who had both attended a coaching skills workshop and been coached now talked about coaching in terms of empowerment and helping people work out what to do for themselves. Those who had only been coached (mostly the senior executives) remained in the coaching-as-telling camp, along with people further down the organization who had neither been coached nor attended a workshop. A fault-line was therefore opening up between the senior executive team and their direct reports (Gover and Duxbury, 2012) and another between the executive's direct reports and others further down the organization.

The coalescing of perspectives into two different camps meant that the organization was no closer to aligning around a true common purpose. For some people the future vision was a world in which leaders spent more time telling people how to do their job more effectively. For others it was a world in which leaders spent more time finding out what motivated their people and empowering them to take more responsibility

Just as perspectives tended to bifurcate, so we saw a possible shift in the identities of some people in the organization. Everyone was still very busy, but some began to express a desire to spend more time developing their people. In effect they were questioning their role as a leader and the extent to which they were fullling that role.

One of the aspects participants most enjoyed about the workshops was the opportunity to engage in dialogue. The workshops mostly grouped people by geography and became a new forum in which people began to discuss some of the ways in which they could improve ways of working together. The OD manager travelled the organization effectively role-modelling this more dialogic way of interacting and coaching others to do the same.

While some people expressed a desire to spend more time developing their people, few appeared to feel empowered to change their behaviour without some signal from above. This included some members of the senior executive. This appeared to be an organization waiting for permission to behave differently, reflecting the formal hierarchy.

The boundaries between different 'coalitions' appeared to be softening. However, with the departure of the OD manager and the completion of the workshops, people seemed worried that there appeared to exist no other forums for effective dialogue. They worried that the work may have come to an end and wondered what were the senior executive team's intentions, in particular the new CEO (Figure 13.5).

A focus on dialogue

The new CEO was excited to hear the outcome of the research that resonated with him in two important ways. First, independent of the ongoing evaluation process, the shareholders of the business had already identified building organizational capability as his most important priority. Second, the observation that an 'expert doer' culture was getting in the way of the development agenda was consistent with his observations that people needed to start prioritizing, and that the executive needed to be the first to role-model this behaviour. The dialogue helped him come to understand the identity of the organization and how that might block the progress of such an agenda.

This was an organization where people ran from meeting to meeting, where there was an unrelenting list of things to do, and in which new people came on board without receiving adequate training and didn't always stay long. Given that there had been a steady flow of people in and out of the organization it was likely that those who were left were those who most enjoyed the adrenalin rush of seeking to get as much done as possible in any one day without stopping for breath. While the senior executive saw this as something their direct reports needed to manage, the research told us that the senior executives were the ones who said they had least time to spend coaching others, and who were probably struggling most. The new CEO could see, therefore, that to succeed in building a coaching culture, or what was best described in this organization as a development culture, two big steps the organization would need to take would be first, to engage in more dialogue and second, to prioritize.

In May the CEO took his executive team away for four days to engage in dialogue. They spent three of those days getting to know one another and listening to one another's perspectives on the business. The CEO and HR director didn't tell the team what the agenda was going to be in advance, because they feared there might be some kind of mass rebellion! But the team came away from the event feeling more cohesive.

A couple of weeks later the HR director assembled the global HR team to review the outcome of the last round of interviews. The team discussed the findings and again explored each other's perspectives as to what was

FIGURE 13.5 Listening to the organization a third time

The fault-lines between the perspectives of senior executive direct reports and other layers of management were still intact but beginning to soften, in that 40 per cent of the senior executive now defined coaching with reference to listening and empowerment, as did 50 per cent of team members.

When asked what an ideal coaching culture would look like, most people spoke not just about people being developed, but also people feeling empowered. This seemed to represent a small shift toward a clearer purpose, perhaps as a consequence of the corresponding shifts in perspectives.

Despite these slight shifts in perspective and purpose, evidence from coaching assignments suggested that the organization remained committed to doing. Workshop participants were worried that the work on coaching would be wasted. Without the OD manager to support them, they had done little themselves to further embed new behaviours and they saw little change in the behaviour of the senior executive. The organization's focus on doing remained core to its identity.

Most of the new forums for dialogue were no longer available. The workshops had come to an end, the OD manager was no longer hosting teleconferences for alumni, and nor was she there to support managers and role-model new behaviours.

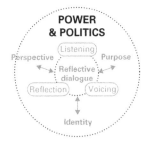

With the CEO and OD manager gone, people wondered what was about to happen next. What was the new CEO like? Would the OD manager be replaced? How would the organization work in the future? How would things get done?

happening in each market. When the team moved later in the day to discussing a vision for the future and a common purpose, they recognized the need to come up with different strategies for different markets, particularly in China. The team left the workshop with a series of actions, mostly on taking the initiative to create more forums for dialogue, and some requests to the senior executive team about creating expectations of managers throughout the organization to spend more time focusing on people's development. They also came up with a series of measures they would use to track progress toward a desired future state.

The emergence of purpose

It is really only at this point, more than a year after the initiative began, that the coaching programme assumed a real purpose, actively supported by the executive and the global HR team. The purpose switched from 'introducing a coaching culture' to building a culture in which people could expect to be developed through being empowered to take more responsibility. Coaching was positioned as a form of conversation that could help the organization achieve that aim; in effect – dialogue.

Using the ECM

This organization may soon succeed in getting to a place where its senior executives spend more time developing their direct reports, who in turn spend more time developing their teams. Leaders may be persuaded to spend less time doing and more time empowering. The organization as a whole may come to appreciate the value of listening in understanding other's needs and aspirations. That won't, however, mean the journey has come to an end. People will continue to leave the organization and new people will come on board. The company will establish new ventures and find that others fail or are sold. There may be another financial crisis of some description, or people may suddenly decide they don't want to buy the company's products any more. The future is unpredictable and things will change.

If the organization is to continue to be successful as it grows it will need to further develop its capacity to change. From a 'programme management' perspective this means that the 'programme' is ongoing; it has no end. The organization will need to continue standing back from itself, reflecting on the quality of the dialogue in which it's engaged, the extent to which it understands itself and to which it has a common purpose moving forwards.

It will need to continue to reflect on its identity and to question that identity.

The linear approach typically has a beginning and an end. A culture is spoken about as if it's a house: something to be constructed and completed. The reality is that a culture lives and breathes through the multitude of conversations that take place around a never ending stream of events. If to declare a culture complete is to believe we no longer need to engage in dialogue, then that is the moment that the ongoing evolution of culture is likely to take a surprising turn without our influence at the heart of the dialogue.

KEY POINTS

- Reflective dialogue sits at the heart of change.

- Eschewing linear models of change, sometimes you just have to get started, even if key stakeholders may not yet be aligned with the way forward. A practical judgement is required based on information available at the time. I expand on this point in Chapter 14.

- One of the key roles of a leader is to engage in dialogue. This is just as important as being seen to visibly advocate a change initiative. I expand on leadership in Chapter 15.

- By applying a reflective framework over a more activities-based change process, we are able to adopt a more systemic approach to managing change. This theme is discussed further in Chapter 16.

- Coaching has a powerful, often unrealized role to play in the management of change programmes because coaching (at least as defined by some people) is in effect the practice of reflective dialogue. The potential role of coaching is discussed in Chapter 17.

Getting started

14

A systemic approach

Looking at the emerging change model again (Figure 14.1) we might consider framing a leadership development agenda around the skills and behaviours of listening, voicing, taking time to reflect and thinking systemically. Building a curriculum around these skills would be consistent with a traditional approach to leadership development, but doesn't feel consistent with the messages emerging from our storytellers. Becoming a better listener appears to be more about being curious and self-aware than it does about learning a new skill. Becoming a more effective speaker seems to be more about courage and being grounded than it does about learning a new technique. Becoming more reflective and thinking systemically are less about

FIGURE 14.1 The emerging change model (ECM)

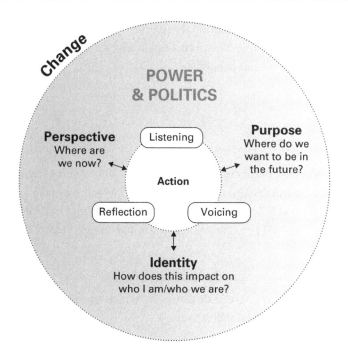

learning a particular reflective process and more about developing the capacity to be both inside and outside the moment at the same time.

How does a leader become more self-aware, grounded and reflective? From the perspective of the emerging change model, this is about individuals, teams and whole organizations becoming more authentic, and authenticity isn't a skill. How can we help facilitate the evolution of authenticity?

The traditional approach to organizational development (OD) is to focus on individuals and their development. This is consistent with what Marshak and Grant (2008) call 'traditional' OD and what Werkman (2010) calls 'classical' OD. The primary focus of the classical OD practitioner is to put in place programmes to facilitate the realization of individual potential, while concurrently reviewing structures, systems and processes that get in the way of that individual potential being realized. Leadership development programmes therefore focus on enhancing the capability of the individual, in other words enhancing the capability of the organization a few people at a time. This highlights another aspect of the traditional approach to organizational development, namely that it isn't very systemic. It doesn't take into account the multitude of other variables that determine how people behave nor the dynamic process through which people are continually re-evaluating their behaviours through their interactions with others.

Chapter 15 explores how we might think differently about leadership, drawing on aspects of the ECM, and Chapter 16 considers a more systemic approach to building organizational capability. Before we move on however, let's first consider a couple of aspects of planning an investment in the development of organizational capability.

Purpose

In the Introduction to this book I cited Burnes (2011) who reviewed a series of change programmes and meta-studies all of which reported failure rates of between 60 and 90 per cent. But what do these numbers really mean? To suggest that about 70 per cent of organizational change efforts fail or disappoint implies:

1 There are always agreed objectives in the first place.

2 There are always agreed measures by which to define the achievement of these objectives.

3 These objectives remain constant.

In practice, as we'll see, few of these conditions are often met, which begs the question – how do people come up with these success and failure rates? Burnes (2011) dissected the papers citing high failure rates and found that they could be sorted into three categories. The first group of writers cited high failure rates without offering any evidence to support their claim. The second group of writers provided anecdotal evidence without any detailed supporting evidence. The third group of writers cited other writers from the first two groups. Hughes (2011) reviewed five change studies in detail, each of which cited a 70 per cent failure rate. In each case he failed to find valid and reliable empirical evidence in support of the espoused 70 per cent rate. Having listened to our storytellers, this comes as no surprise. Hughes wouldn't find any 'valid' or 'reliable' evidence in this study of any particular rate of success/failure.

We began our interviews asking our storytellers to think of two stories: a successful change intervention, which we asked them to recount first, and an unsuccessful intervention, to speak about if we had time. We didn't offer any definition as to what might constitute success and failure. Many of our storytellers had to think for a while as to what constituted success. One interviewee even said, 'Let me tell you the story and then we can decide if it was successful or not.'

Listening to the stories it became clear that different people often come to different conclusions regarding the success or failure of an initiative. One of our storytellers was charged with replacing a legacy IT system. The task proved complex, with different stakeholder groups seeking to advance different agendas. In the end the system was replaced, but was the programme successful?

> A lot of people said the programme was a success, because we implemented a
> new system which worked well, but for me it wasn't successful. It became
> a battleground, with winners and losers, which in retrospect didn't have to
> happen.

To be able to classify change interventions as successful or otherwise, every change programme needs to have a clear definition of success and every important stakeholder needs to subscribe to that definition. In practice this appears to be rarely the case. One of our external practitioners said:

> A business case needs to be developed with the change in mind and the people
> who are going to be affected need to be engaged before you start. It fails when
> those instigating the change haven't thought hard enough about what they
> want. People are often too Pollyanna-ish when they start; they think no one

will be worried. Organizations which are really successful are good at defining the change. They have lead indicators not lag indicators so they can adjust their approach if they're not progressing.

One task of the change practitioner is to facilitate this alignment between different people with different perspectives who may be difficult to engage in meaningful, effective dialogue. As the case study in Chapter 13 illustrated, aligning people around a common purpose is often the most difficult aspect of any change process, yet it is when attempting to align others that we find out more about the quality of dialogue to which the organization is committed.

Getting started

To be able to demonstrate the success or failure of a programme therefore requires clarity of purpose. This is easier said than done. If we think back to the case study in Chapter 13, the CEO couldn't articulate a clear purpose for the programme before it started. He found the question difficult to answer, which isn't untypical. If I think about leadership development programmes, for example, many executives, when asked, 'What is the purpose of this programme?' would answer something like, 'To enhance the capability of our leaders', a generic purpose which isn't particularly useful either in helping us design an intervention or in helping us decide whether our efforts have been successful.

If we set off with a generic purpose such as 'to enhance the capability of our leaders' then it's likely that we'll source a generic definition of leadership from which to build a generic leadership programme. To measure the effectiveness of our programme we might build in some behavioural assessments, so we can show how our investment has led to measurable changes in those behaviours. The problem with this approach is that there may be no evident link between the change in behaviours we have encouraged and the ability of the business to address the challenges it faces in seeking to achieve its strategy. Contrast this to a scenario in which the executive are aligned around a clear definition of what they hope to see happen as a consequence of an investment in change leadership.

About 12 years ago I led the design and implementation of a leadership development programme for a global multinational. The programme was built for a target population of more than 12,000 leaders, and we reported to a steering committee of four group vice-presidents. About halfway through the programme the organization decided it needed to undergo a round of significant cost reductions in order to achieve the group's financial targets for the year. Alongside most of the group's activities, the leadership programme came under threat. To preserve the programme we suggested to the steering committee that we tweak the agenda of the programme to support leaders in meeting their cost-reduction targets. The idea was firmly knocked back with one of the GVPs declaring with great conviction that his main hope for the programme overall was that it was helping leaders across the company to manage ambiguity and uncertainty more effectively and that he didn't want to put at risk the effectiveness of the programme in this regard by focusing on externally imposed short-term cost reductions. Managing ambiguity wasn't one of the official objectives of the programme, nor did it show up as one of the organization's stated leadership competencies, but it helped us think anew about how to measure the success of the programme.

The importance of establishing the purpose of an intervention upfront is consistent with the content of many traditional linear approaches to change. The problem is that people often find it difficult to express what the purpose of a programme is. In the case study in Chapter 13 the CEO couldn't precisely articulate the purpose of the coaching skills programme. I suggested that we could have done a better job in eliciting the purpose of the programme earlier, but I don't know that we would have succeeded. In the event it was the outcome of the work itself that helped the executive to clarify the purpose of the programme. The same may be said of the leadership programme I have just described. The programme had been going for about 18 months at the time, and much of the anecdotal feedback we received was about how helpful some people found it in helping them become more effective at a time when the company was embarked upon a long and intense series of mergers and acquisitions. As Lewin once said (Burnes, 2004), 'one cannot understand an organization without trying to change it'.

Establishing the purpose of an investment in capability is important then. But we don't always have access to key stakeholders to ask them what that purpose is, nor would we always find it easy to facilitate an alignment around that purpose. The ECM tells us that purpose is often emergent and that to facilitate its emergence we must create the space for effective dialogue. We then need to remain in that dialogue as the environment changes and the purpose shifts and changes accordingly.

KEY POINTS

- To help leaders and organizations to become more capable of leading change we must help them to become more authentic.

- Traditional approaches to leadership and organizational development are individualistic and don't usually take into account the social aspects of complexity and meaning-making.

- There is little evidence to support the notion that 70 per cent of organizational change efforts fail or disappoint, partly because it is rare for key stakeholders to align around key metrics.

- Aligning key stakeholders around a common purpose is not a one-off event. It may take time for a common purpose to emerge, and that purpose is likely to evolve over time.

Leadership

In the last chapter I contrasted two approaches to enhancing change leadership capability. With reference to the emerging change model, a traditional approach may focus on skills, such as listening, voicing, reflecting and thinking systemically. I contrasted that with an approach focused on facilitating the growth of self-awareness and authenticity. In this chapter I'll build on the significance of authenticity and consider what implications the ECM may have for how we think about leadership.

Complexity and the role of practical judgement

Schön (1991) talks about a crisis of confidence in the professions. Most professions establish knowledge criteria for people wanting to practise within that domain. Doctors, for example, must demonstrate that they know how to treat particular diseases according to the methods endorsed by their professional institutions. The prevailing assumption is that a body of knowledge can be compiled that will present the professional with an appropriate response to every situation she is likely to face. In many professions today, however, practitioners are coming across more and more examples where traditional methods prove ineffective. As a metaphor this serves well for thinking about leadership.

An approach to leadership development based only on the teaching of skills and models reflects the same perspective. Underpinning this approach is an implicit assumption that we can distil all of the different issues a leader is likely to face into a limited number of standard scenarios. Thus we might expect to see leadership texts defining a generic set of skills which between them cover all these scenarios. There are lots of books and assessment tools providing a holistic definition of what it is to be a leader in terms of skills, competencies and behaviours. Accordingly most leadership competency frameworks look similar because they are sourced from the same literature base and the same set of assumptions. Leaders are encouraged to refer to these generic frameworks and to learn standard approaches to dealing with everyday situations. Stacey (2012) goes so far as to suggest that leadership programmes teach 'institutionalized techniques of discipline'. He says:

> I would argue that today's leaders are the agents of discipline in society and the process of training large numbers of managers as leaders is a key activity sustaining the disciplinary society. Leadership and leadership development programmes are far more about order and discipline than they are about change and creativity.

He goes so far as to say:

> Most leadership programmes provide examples of doublethink. They claim to be about how the leader should bring about change, but they really amount to the corrective training required to sustain the status quo.

As Stacey points out, there is nothing wrong with regarding leaders as the agents of order and discipline. Organizations need order and discipline and leaders are the obvious candidates to manage it. What he is in effect suggesting is that while leaders may be asked both to instil order and discipline *and* to lead change, the environment or system within which they operate may be more conducive to the first task than the latter. In Chapter 8 we considered the different ways in which middle management are engaged in change. Sometimes, it appears, their role is restricted to implementing what they have been told to implement without being engaged in the creative process. On other occasions they may have a role to play in the creative process, a step that would appear to greatly enhance the likelihood that the rest of the organization will engage in the kind of dialogue required to generate coordinated change.

We are asking two things of our leaders then: to administer, maintain and coordinate, and to create. In dealing with complex change the skills of administration, maintenance and coordination are unlikely to suffice. There are no books or courses that can alone provide the leader with a prescribed set of solutions for each and every situation they are likely to face. The world is too complex to be able to define standard solutions to generic problems, and if we do seek to rely upon the judgement of 'experts' we are likely to discover quite frequently that those judgements are wrong. Because models and tools cannot be relied upon the leader must exercise what Stacey calls 'practical judgement', ie judgement acquired through experience and reflection upon that experience. This is not to say that skills don't matter, rather it is to say that no one can tell us in advance of a particular dilemma which skill to apply, how to tailor it to circumstance, nor how to respond should the consequences not align with our expectations. This 'practical judgement' is not a matter of theoretical application, but a matter of self-knowledge, trial and error, experience and reflection.

Strategy

Now is a good time to talk about strategy. I sometimes hear people talk about strategy as if it were independent of change management; that change management is a process that kicks in after a strategy has been decided. Strategizing is often depicted as a purely cerebral activity, all about models and logical thinking. I would argue that effective strategizing is no less an outcome of practical judgement than any other aspect of change.

In the Introduction to this book I said that most texts on change suggest that around 70 per cent of change efforts fail or disappoint (though I challenged this in Chapter 14). In the world of strategy we come across similar numbers. An oft-cited article by Charan and Colvin, published in a 1999 edition of *Fortune*, suggests that CEOs fail because of strategy implementation: 'In the majority of cases – we estimate 70 per cent – the real problem isn't the high-concept boners the boffins love to talk about. It's bad execution.'

In response it seems that many strategists have followed the example of traditional change managers and focused on coming up with better tools and methodologies. Kaplan and Norton (2000), for example, suggest that strategy implementation fails because people don't understand the strategy. The answer therefore is to 'map' the change creating a clear picture of cause and effect for people to refer to and understand. Alternatively, and contrary to what Charan and Colvin appear to be suggesting, it may not be that execution *per se* is the problem, so much as the mindset in which strategy creation and execution are seen as distinct and sequential.

Mintzberg and Ansoff engaged in a fascinating exchange of letters back in the early 1990s. The debate began when Mintzberg (1990) wrote an article critiquing the premise that strategy formulation is a process of carefully controlled thought. This is not how strategy happens in practice, he claimed. He likened strategic change to stepping out into the unknown, and framed strategy as a learning process in which thinking and acting go hand in hand. Ansoff (1991) responded vigorously, suggesting that Mintzberg's claims were based on a limited understanding of the corporate context. Mintzberg responded in turn with reference to strategy formulation at Honda which, he said, successfully captured two-thirds of the US motorcycle market through embarking on a process of do-learn-do, ignoring the grand strategy recommended to it by a consulting firm. Said Mintzberg:

> We think we are so awfully smart. We can work it all out in advance, so cleverly, we 'rational' human beings... We can predict the future, identify the non-starters, impose our minds on all that matter... Of course we need to think. Of course we want to be rational. But it's a [complex*] world out there. We all know that we shall get nowhere without emergent learning alongside deliberate planning.

(*Mintzberg uses the word 'complicated', though I think he would have used the word 'complex' as defined in this book.)

Strategy in these terms cannot be formulated independent of the change process. I'm reminded of a conversation I had more than 15 years ago with someone who worked at the heart of a global multinational. We walked across the floor where the global 'strategy' teams worked while he explained that what these people actually did was attempt to manage the interface between senior executive performance expectations and what was actually happening out in the businesses. Strategy formulation, he said, is what happens when senior executives engage in dialogue with each other and with others in the organization. In reality then, as Mintzberg suggests, action and thought go hand in hand, and the real work of strategy happens in the dialogue around events. At some point leaders may feel they have the strategy 'right', but the point at which an organization moves into implementation is not the time to withdraw from dialogue. The effective 'strategist' remains committed to dialogue and remains curious as to how the strategy will continue to evolve and emerge.

Authentic leadership

The emerging change model encourages us to focus on authenticity rather than skills. This is not to say that there is no place for teaching people new skills; rather it is to say that what characterizes the effective change leader from the less effective leader is not just knowledge. The biggest differentiator, I would argue, is authenticity. Authenticity underpins the leader's capacity to listen, to effectively voice and to reflect and think systemically.

Listening

In Chapter 3 I positioned listening as the key differentiator between monologue and dialogue. We considered different forms of listening and how hard it can be to listen to someone without filtering her words through our own agenda. To pay attention to the meaning that the other person is attempting to convey and to seek to understand the origins of that meaning requires being authentically curious. It requires silencing our own judgements, and being conscious of a natural predilection for selectively listening for what seems to best fit our existing perspective. This kind of curiosity is authentic in that it depends on the listener genuinely believing that she might learn something new and valuable by listening outside her own point of view. To be able to listen outside our own point of view means we need to understand the origins of our own perspective, to able to regard it systemically.

Voicing

In Chapter 4 I suggested that fear is often a barrier to effective voicing. This may be the fear of looking stupid, the fear of being challenged or being asked difficult questions, or the fear of being excluded from future discussions. Effective voicing is courageous. This courage, I argued in Chapter 10, is linked to authenticity, in that people who are more self-aware are more likely to have confidence in their own judgement.

Reflection

The self-aware leader is more likely to see the world systemically and to habitually switch continuously from being in the moment to standing outside the moment and back again. The systemic perspective means that leaders are less likely to feel quite so attached to their agenda in the moment, because they are aware of its origins and the likelihood that other, equally valid, agendas are likely to exist. The effective change leader therefore feels compelled to try and view any given situation from multiple angles. The effective change leader is not afraid of being uncertain, or of expressing a view amid that uncertainty. Reflection, in this sense, is not about spending half an hour a week thinking about what has gone before; rather it is a mindset, a constant way of being.

Spotting the authentic leader

How can we tell if someone is 'authentic'? It may be useful here to think back to Chapter 10 and the idea that authenticity is not the same thing as sincerity. When people are being sincere they are focused on trying to articulate as best they can what they are thinking and feeling. This is not the same as being authentic. Sincerity and authenticity may look much the same in the moment. However, the authentic person is speaking with a more informed sense of who she is. Her message is likely to be more consistent, more enduring and more energetic over time.

Reflecting on the ECM, two traits to look for in an authentic leader are courage and a desire to listen, or 'fearless curiosity'. If I think of the two or three leaders in my early career that seemed special to me, one quality they all had was a wonderful sense of being present. These people were busy, yet in their presence it seemed like their whole attention was being directed at me. I was conscious that every word I spoke was being listened to in an environment of respect. I found myself listening hard to every word I uttered myself, knowing that if I said something careless, any flaw in my argument would be duly noted. At the same time I didn't feel I was on trial. I felt an absence of anxiety in the person I was speaking to and a sense that the conversation was in essence a development opportunity for me, a chance to test myself and to be availed of feedback as to how I was progressing.

Fearless curiosity is different to curiosity without courage. Being spoken to by someone in authority who lacks courage can feel like being on trial. Every word the person utters appears to be processed against an inflexible set of criteria and any deviance from these criteria invokes fear, for if others are not seeing the world the way she sees it, it means she is not in control. Curiosity here is about self-protection, being alert for signs of danger, and the fear of the leader is often manifested in the form of anger. Fearless curiosity is also different to courage without curiosity. The fearless leader who doesn't stop to listen may appear charismatic on the surface but is unlikely to lead the organization to success.

How does the fearlessly curious leader approach complexity? Reflecting on the ECM it seems to me there is a fundamental difference between developing a tolerance for ambiguity and embracing ambiguity as something to relish and enjoy. If we don't enjoy complexity then it becomes something to be endured. This would appear to frame the life of the leader as being necessarily stressful. A language of 'tolerance to ambiguity' or 'resilience' makes sense if we're operating from a primary desire for certainty and control, but it implies a regret that change isn't more straightforward and easy to manage. This is a different mindset to a cheerful acceptance that complexity is the norm and is always interesting and mysterious. The less authentic leader is unlikely to feel curious, for the more she explores complexity and its unknowns, the more uncertain life becomes. The biggest barrier to curiosity in the less authentic leader may be the fear that she will become even more uncertain. Resilience for the less authentic leader means adorning a bullet-proof jacket. Resilience for the more authentic leader means feeling confident and grounded.

It's not easy to remain fearlessly curious when working in an environment in which control and certainty are highly valued. It demands a different way of looking at the world. Remember what one of our storytellers said:

> If the numbers falter they may hang me out to dry. That's a personal risk, but it's not my career – it's a job. If I was trying to be a corporate guy then I couldn't take risks. I used to work in private equity where your job is it; you sell the business, you lose your job. That's a good mindset to have at the senior level. I'm not here to make them happy, but to do the right thing. It's a very liberating mental attitude.

Fearlessly curious leaders are committed to learning. Because change is constant and ongoing, they know that what worked before may not work next time. They reflect because they are curious to understand the impact of their actions, the dynamics of their team, the mechanics of their organizations, and how the impact, dynamics and mechanics change and evolve in response to ongoing change.

One of our storytellers managed a complex investment scenario in China, working with shareholders from different countries and different factions within China itself. When I asked him to what he attributed his success, he said:

> I just love learning and finding out what I don't know. I'm very enthusiastic and energetic; I get revved up by the people I'm working with and I like having lots of balls in the air. That's the way I'm wired; otherwise I get bored. The China thing was very complex, but it was an environment I enjoyed because of its complexity.

Another of our storytellers, an internal practitioner, spoke about what she felt she had learnt about leadership:

> Being able to be a great leader requires self-awareness and flexibility. As leaders become more self-aware, they become more capable and robust. Great leaders need to be awesome learners.

Traditional leadership development programmes don't appear well crafted to cultivate this fearless curiosity. Leadership tends to be framed in terms of generic skills and competencies, techniques to be learnt and applied. Such programmes by themselves are unlikely to be effective in a world of complex change. So how else might we structure such interventions?

KEY POINTS

- One role of the leader is to maintain control and discipline; another is to lead people through the complexity of change, a process that can't be controlled.

- While the change leader may value learning new skills in service of leading change, skills alone are unlikely to be sufficient.

- The effective change leader is relatively authentic. This may show up as 'fearless curiosity'.

- Effective change leaders are on a mission to become more self-aware, and more aware of their surroundings.

Building capability

16

In Chapter 14 we began to think about how to build the capability of the organization to change itself. The traditional approach tends to be individualistic, focused on building the skills of its leaders one by one. This approach may not be effective if it focuses too much on skills and not enough on mindset, and not if the approach is overly individualistic. The effective change leader is authentic, which manifests itself in something we might call 'fearless curiosity'. So how do we go about helping our *organizations* become more fearlessly curious, more authentic?

If we consider again the emerging change model, we notice once more that effective dialogue sits at the heart of change. This says if we want our

FIGURE 16.1 The emerging change model (ECM)

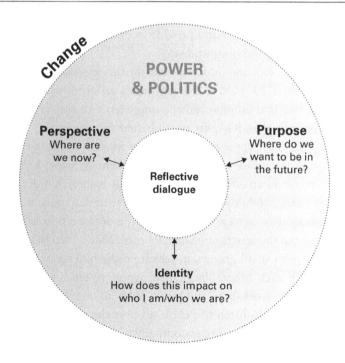

organizations to become better at change, we need to enhance the collective capacity of the organization to engage in reflective dialogue.

The role of the change agent

As I write this chapter I'm coming to the end of a series of interviews with Australian HR directors and OD managers, asking them about their experiences of change. One spoke about the importance of courageous leadership in effecting change, and of the energy required to engage with people who may be invested in their own personal agendas. It's not enough, she said, to send out e-mails and memos to staff. People want to understand the context and people have questions about doing the best job they can. To steer people though change, she said, requires an enormous amount of skill, the ability to engage, listen and to 'take account of'. She then spoke about her own organization and said that few leaders there have the capacity to engage in effective dialogue. She spoke about one division in particular, whose success depended upon the ability of its leadership to accurately gauge what others within the division were thinking. The trouble was that the two most senior people in the leadership team didn't engage in dialogue, they didn't go and talk to their business and as a consequence didn't seem to know what was going on. It was up to her and her team, she said, to be the 'pulse', to engage in dialogue with the division and provide feedback to the team leaders in a 'balanced and useful and insightful way'.

This resonated with me as I reflected on the sequence of events summarized in Chapter 13. Had the organization adhered to a linear change methodology, one that emphasized the importance of buy-in at the beginning of the process, then it's quite possible that the executive would still be stuck in a 'Catch-22', expressing the desire to see people engage in dialogue about personal development without having themselves got a place where they could engage in an effective dialogue about having that dialogue! The advocates of change didn't wait for the executive to determine a compelling purpose; instead they went about engaging the organization in a dialogue. In the early part of the programme the OD manager decided to run coaching skills workshops in small groups, in which people had the space to engage in dialogue with each other. She invited people to engage in further dialogue following the workshop, and put in place an ongoing evaluation process that enabled me to listen to people all over the organization. The new HR director took up the baton, encouraging the new CEO to focus on the quality of dialogue between members of his team, and continuing to support the ongoing evaluation process.

From my conversation with the Australian OD manager emerged Figure 16.2. This diagram charts the progress of an organization from a scenario in which there are no structured opportunities for people to engage in dialogue. This doesn't mean that dialogue doesn't happen; the ECM is a depiction of how change happens anyway – people will engage in dialogue whether we want them to or not. It means that dialogue is happening below the radar screen, in Schön's swampy lowlands (Beech *et al*, 2011). It usually means that the company's leadership aren't engaged in a dialogue with the rest of the organization or even, sometimes, with each other. The circle on the right depicts a scenario in which leaders are engaged in dialogue and in which they have created forums for dialogue.

How to get from A to C? Our thoughts may go straight to a structured development programme focused on enhancing leadership capability, but designing and implementing such programmes takes time. Furthermore, such a strategy may not prove successful if executed in isolation from the broader organizational system. In the meantime the business has decisions to make and the world keeps changing. To influence change therefore, change advocates (often, but not always HR) must step in and initiate the dialogue themselves. It's important this is done within a systemic frame with the bigger picture in mind. By initiating dialogue the change agent creates the opportunity for others to engage in dialogue and thereby come to appreciate the value of dialogue. This is not to suggest that change agents attempt to assume personal responsibility for the effectiveness of dialogue across the whole organization; rather it is to suggest that a systemic approach to building capability will be multi-faceted and that change advocates have a direct role to play.

If we adhere to a model that says for a change programme to work leaders must buy-in to change when they don't have the capacity to engage in effective dialogue about that change, we'll be stuck at first base for a long time. This model posits a role for HR, or any other change agency, to begin building capability by creating the space for dialogue. This in itself provides leaders with the opportunity to experience dialogue and to understand its value both in achieving change and becoming more effective and authentic leaders. So the immediate focus of the internal practitioner may be to establish dialogic processes within the organization. This is likely to include playing some of the roles of the effective change leader, such as 'management by walking about' and simply engaging people in dialogue about what's going on in the organization, people's hopes for the future of the organization, and

FIGURE 16.2 Building capability to lead change

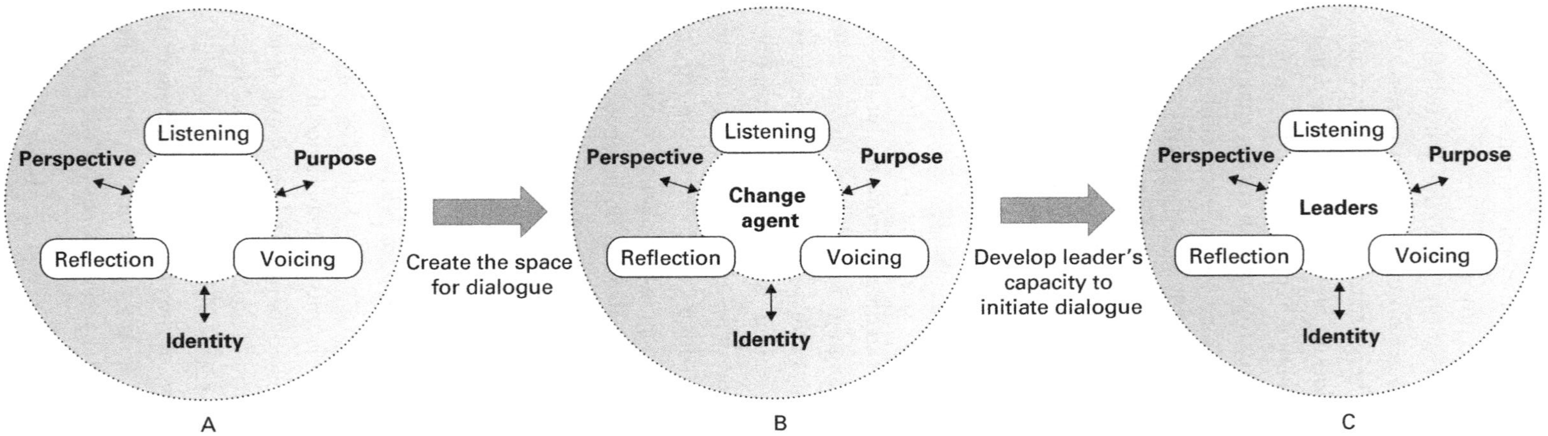

some of things that are important to them. The internal practitioner is then in a position to act as a conduit between the leadership of the organization and the rest of its membership, providing feedback and advice, role-modelling effective dialogue in the process. This isn't a role that HR, or any other function, is going to want to play for very long. The change agent needs to be simultaneously focused on developing the leadership of the organization so that it becomes capable of engaging in effective dialogue without always being prompted or supported.

The model in Figure 16.2 is, of course, not linear! If we think back to the case study in Chapter 13, the original change advocate was the OD manager, who took us from point A to point B. The OD manager then left the organization and for a few months we were arguably back at point A. In some organizations the impetus for dialogue may come from the leadership themselves, such that the organization goes from point A to point C. The value of Figure 16.2 is in illustrating the benefits of sitting back and reflecting on who is deliberately engineering dialogue at any point in time in service of charting a systemic approach to building capability.

Becoming more authentic

Authenticity is about becoming more self-aware and more aware of how to engage effectively with others. To become more aware requires being curious. It requires seeking out new experiences, new opportunities to reflect and learn, and more feedback. By becoming more aware individuals, teams and organizations become more confident as to who they are, of their identities. This increased confidence bestows more courage to seek out new challenges and so on. As discussed in Chapter 8, all of us have multiple identities: as leader, as team member, as partner, parent and so on. We have individual and collective identities. Figure 16.3 shows both processes for the evolution of individual and collective authenticity.

The traditional OD paradigm focuses on the development of the individual, but through a systemic lens we can see how this may be ineffective. The implicit assumption underlying individualistic approaches to leadership development is that we create our own identities. The task therefore is to take the individual, help him become clearer as to who he wants to be, before sending him back into the organizational environment where he will naturally be more effective. The reality is that change happens anyway, and that we co-create our identities through dialogue with others. In the organizational environment I am constantly reviewing my identity, based on my experiences in the workplace and my reflection upon those events with other

FIGURE 16.3 Authenticity, curiosity and confidence

I learn from those reflections and become more confident about who I am

I want to know more about me

Authenticity

I want to reflect on those experiences to find out more about me

I want to find out by experiencing myself doing new things

Individual perspective

We learn from those reflections and become more confident about who we are

We want to know more about us

Authenticity

We want to reflect on those experiences to find out more about us

We want to find out by experiencing us doing new things

Collective perspective

people. To take someone out of that 'system' and place them in a different 'system' may lead to a change in identity, but that change is likely to be short-lived once the individual is dropped back into the system within which he works on a day-to-day basis.

For example, I might be concerned about my ability to engage with others. I go to a leadership development course where I'm introduced to some new models for engaging people, which include paying more attention to what others have to say. I discuss the model with the facilitators and fellow participants. The facilitators speak passionately about the value of listening to others, and my fellow participants appear persuaded. We speak about the models in between sessions and agree with each other that these new approaches make sense and that we'll seek to incorporate these new behaviours into our role as leaders.

On Monday I walk straight into the latest crisis. Someone has taken their eye off the ball and as a consequence we have a problem that needs to be fixed. A team meeting has been called to determine next steps. Everyone is stressed and everyone has a different opinion on what needs to happen next, though just about all are agreed that the team needs to step in and start delivering instructions on how to sort things out. At this point I suggest we refrain from an immediate intervention and take the time to ask people closer to the situation what they think has happened. The rest of the team stare at me as if I've just been on a leadership course and explain why time is of the essence, and how it's the leadership team's role to step in and intervene when things go wrong. Suitably chastised, but still doubtful, I later share my thoughts with my line manager, who persuades me of the value of decisive leadership.

This isn't to say there isn't room for workshop-style learning. Rather it is to say that the systemic practitioner instigates a portfolio of activities, formal and informal, at the individual and collective levels, and charts the progress of these activities and the links between them.

Working with groups and teams

If our purpose is to develop more authentic organizations and to develop the capacity of leadership across the board to lead change more effectively, then it makes sense to direct more of our development budget to working with groups and teams. Bringing people together in groups and teams will not in itself result in capability development. What's important is that programmes focus on dialogue. People are encouraged to engage in dialogue themselves, and to reflect on the function of dialogue.

I believe that more developmental resource will be directed toward working with intact teams in the future as people come to appreciate a more systemic perspective of change and the potential for learning inherent in every working team. Teams are complex entities. Kantor (2012), for example, talks about the 'structural dynamics' of human interaction, the idea that there is an underlying structure and a set of ongoing patterns in the way we relate to each other. Most of us, Kantor says, pay attention to what people say and how they say it when we work with others in a team. We may agree or disagree with content and find ourselves align or disengage with others based on their style. Few of us pay attention to the structure underlying our exchanges: the implicit rules and assumptions that drive our behaviour and the patterns that emerge as a result. This is an incredibly rich and fertile ground for leaders to practise operating from a new balcony, and a manageable step for those seeking to work with the complex dynamics operating across an organization.

Some people dismiss the value of teamwork on the basis that teams are forever forming and reforming. Where is the value in helping a team become more effective if that team then disbands? From a systemic perspective it makes no difference whether the team is likely to disband or not. The processes through which people come and go are often some of the most illuminating aspects of a team for people to explore and understand. Not only does teamwork constitute an opportunity for the leader of that team to learn how to instigate change through others, it is also an opportunity for every other member of the team to develop a greater sense of awareness as to the systemic nature of change, and their role in contributing to that change. It is an opportunity for everyone to reflect on the value of effective dialogue, and how to address some of the barriers to it. It's also an opportunity for people to refine and review their models of effective leadership together. In this way people from within the organization have the opportunity to contribute to the development of other's leadership identities, making it more likely that the organization as a whole will develop a strong collective identity. The outcome of this kind of work is usually a more purposeful team, able to engage in honest and open dialogue with itself, and to manage its own transitions through different episodes of its organizational life. It also results in the individuals on that team developing a heightened awareness of how teams work, the value of dialogue and how to address the 'structural dynamics' of other relationships in which they are engaged.

Working with groups is also useful. Here I'm using the word 'team' to mean a collective working toward a common goal, the achievement of which means team members must work together effectively. That might be a formal team or a project team, brought together to achieve a short-term outcome. A group is a collective of people who work in different parts of the organization in different teams. If they have a collective purpose it is likely to be high level, a purpose shared by the organization as a whole. Bringing a group together provides the opportunity for people to learn from each other, to contribute to each other's development and to the evolution of each other's leadership identities, and to initiate dialogue across different parts of the organization. This construct can be a very helpful way of reframing 'individual' learning.

Learning together

If I invite 20 people from around the organization to participate in a leadership workshop, is this group learning or individual learning? If I regard it as individual learning then I may not attend to the importance of dialogue and reflection. These are the kinds of workshops that are so packed with content that there is little opportunity for people to make sense of the content together. There may be little emphasis placed on bringing people together in the evenings informally; instead people go home, or spend time alone catching up on their e-mails. If we regard such workshops as group learning then it radically affects our approach to design. Bringing people together to learn together is potentially very powerful. To get it right, in the context of building change capability, means focusing on a few key principles.

1. Establish a clear purpose

Most leadership programmes are based on what appears at first glance to be a clear purpose, namely an intention to develop more leaders within the organization. However, this generic intent doesn't always serve to galvanize leaders to become better leaders, nor does it always motivate senior people in the organization to support the development of participants, and nor does it always lead to observable outcomes that make a difference to the business's success. What's often missing is a robust narrative about the organization and the challenges it's facing, and how those challenges relate to the context of the programme. A more effective purpose might read, for example, 'In the context of this organization's need to grow the business rapidly, we need to develop our collective capacity to engage in effective dialogue across functions.' Notice how the second, more specific, purpose provides clear guidance to the programme designer. For example:

- An articulation of a desired outcome that lends itself to being measured.
- Some guidance as to who to invite.
- Some clues as to how to structure the intervention, in terms of making sure there is plenty of time provided for reflective dialogue.
- A clear idea of what particular skills and abilities to focus on.

However much effort is expended on aligning key stakeholders around an initial purpose, this purpose may change as the organization and its environment change. We must therefore evaluate the outcomes of our work on an ongoing basis.

2. Ongoing evaluation

I did some work recently with an organization that designed a programme to build the capability of its leaders, with a particular emphasis on building engagement. About the time the programme started the organization embarked upon a series of radical restructures designed to rebuild the business model in the face of new competition. The purpose of the programme shifted to one whereby leaders were supported in managing wide-scale structural change.

I worked with another organization a few years ago whose senior leadership team were all approaching retirement age at about the same time. It built a programme with the intention of accelerating the development of high potentials. This government organization was then merged with another, which triggered a long period of doubt and uncertainty. Though the official purpose of the programme remained the same, ongoing evaluation revealed that most participants changed their goals and intentions, focusing their leadership efforts on successfully managing the transition.

The purpose of these kinds of interventions often changes, whether it is the purpose of the programme sponsor or the purpose of the participants. This isn't simply about checking in with sponsors to see what they want the purpose to be. Sense-making is a social process, and the experience of participants may not match the original expectations. That is not to say participants may be disappointed, rather that their experience may simply be different. For example, I'm working with an organization at the moment that built a leadership programme with the intention of imparting particular skills to its middle managers. Ongoing evaluation revealed that participants said they derived most value from learning from each other those approaches directly relevant to the situations they faced, rather than generic skills and models from the facilitator. This insight enabled the organization to review the structure of the programme to further leverage this aspect of the design.

3. Build in reflective dialogue around action

If effective change leadership is about 'practical judgement' (Chapter 15) and authentic leadership can be learnt only through experience and the act of reflecting upon that experience, then we must create experience-rich environments in which people can learn, or structure learning around the work. This is the story of a programme in which leadership development was structured around the work:

> We knew we needed to support an emergent process, not event-based learning. We focused initially on front-line leaders. We worked on relationships and themes around authority, not just 101 stuff. It wasn't role-play – people were working with emergent issues. People found their voices and began discussing the undiscussables. They started to work with conflict. We created the space to have real conversations and for people to craft their own destiny. The results were tangible, and the executive became increasingly committed to it. At the beginning they supported it, but on their site visits they heard about it all the time and said they wanted some of it for themselves, even though it was pretty confrontational. We listened deeply to the organization rather than us starting with a predefined idea of what they needed to learn.

By contrast many leadership development programmes end up so full of predetermined content that dialogue and reflection time get squeezed. One challenge for programme designers is that participants may in effect co-create these content-rich programmes. Some people come to programmes seeking models. They value certainty and control and are looking for solutions. They like the idea that the world is complicated and not complex. They don't see the value in reflective dialogue and view time spent talking as a waste.

4. Encourage systemic thinking

As discussed in Chapter 12, systemic thinking is a process without parameters, a process by which change leaders seek to make sense of the world by taking time to stand aside from the business of doing to reflect on events from different vantage points. There are many ways of encouraging systemic thinking. Asking the group to engage with each other in dialogue may open people's minds to the perspectives of others. Inviting people to reflect may open people's minds to the possibilities of viewing a scenario from different balconies. Bringing the tension between doing and reflecting on that doing to people's awareness is useful. Packing a programme full of models, delivered with the unspoken assumption that tackling change is about following sequential processes, is neither likely to be helpful nor to help people think systemically.

Application

These guidelines ought to help the programme designer avoid some of the following common pitfalls.

Rigorous adherence to leadership competency frameworks

Leadership competency frameworks don't tend to differ from each other very much because they are sourced from the same vast literature base and built on the assumption that the same set of generic skills is required in most circumstances. Generic frameworks tend to encourage generic content that may serve to overconceptualize the learning experience, distancing learning from the work context. A better approach is to frame learning around issues that matter.

A few years ago I led a piece of work where we sought to evaluate the impact of a large-scale global leadership programme. Rather than design the programme around the existing leadership competency framework, we asked the organization what it needed. Once we had been running the programme for about 18 months we went out to the organization again. We asked people all over the organization, a) what behaviours were most important for the level of leadership we were studying, and b) what changes in those behaviours people had noticed. The behaviours people named bore little relation to the official leadership competency framework.

Overemphasizing the value of theory and models

Some workshops are full of theory and models and devoid of reflective dialogue. This is a monological approach in which the facilitator's principal role is to voice. Often the content may make logical sense, but may not make immediate practical sense to the participant. Building exercises into the design and providing an opportunity to receive feedback helps bring theoretical material to life, but participants also need the opportunity to ask questions and to integrate new approaches into their current models for getting things done. This is not simply about having the opportunity to ask the facilitator to clarify something; it is about having the opportunity to discuss content with colleagues, to ask questions of each other and to make sense together. Reflective dialogue must be honoured as an essential component of a programme design, not just seen as a nice-to-have.

Too much task

I see a lot of programmes these days featuring on-the-job projects. Managers are asked to work together to complete a project and to report the results of their efforts to the executive. The idea is that people use the project to try out new behaviours and to reflect on the outcome of those behaviours with fellow project team members. In practice the project often becomes an end in itself, with participants reverting to a habitual focus on getting the task done. The priority becomes putting up a good show in front of senior managers. The original purpose of the project gets lost and teams spend limited time, if any time at all, reflecting on their learning.

Inviting the wrong people

According to our model, effective change leaders are curious. They learn through seeking out new experiences and reflecting on the outcome of their actions. This means that to be interesting, the learning programme must represent a new experience. People won't enjoy listening to new ideas if they can't see the link between them and the challenges they face in the workplace. They won't enjoy a project unless they see how it is going to stretch them in a way they want to be stretched. So in bringing people together to participate in a group learning experience the programme designer must look for people who are curious and eager to learn. Some people are inherently curious and others are not. Those who are not are unlikely to make effective change leaders. However, curiosity is also a function of context and circumstance. People asked to transition into a challenging new role, for example, are likely to be curious, keen to learn new ways of doing things. This is a different frame to the one that says we need to teach a particular new set of skills to everyone at a certain level of the organization. This kind of 'sheep-dip' approach is unlikely to be effective unless there is a compelling collective purpose that engages everyone's curiosity. Without it we may be better off seeking to connect with the curious; those who have a reputation for listening to others and attempting to speak up, who appear open to doing things differently, who constantly seek feedback and who ask to participate.

Not enough time spent reflecting on the outcome

The most common method of programme evaluation is to ask participants after a workshop the extent to which they found it useful. This might entail filling in a form or talking to people soon afterwards. Because a lot of people come to such programmes expecting models and tools, many such programmes are initially well received. The well-documented problem with such approaches is that the extent to which participants enjoy a workshop doesn't appear to correlate particularly well to the likelihood that people will ultimately change their behaviour or adopt a new skill (Arthur *et al*, 2003). Ongoing evaluation is required to discover how people have experienced the learning event and how this learning translates back into the workplace.

It's hard to see how we can come to understand the value of a learning intervention without spending some time exploring the impact systemically. Yet I am still constantly surprised how many organizations choose not to evaluate programmes in this way for lack of resource and time. Given how much is invested in some of these interventions, this seems a peculiarly monologic way of going about things. Organizations are complex and we cannot predict with confidence the impact of any specific learning intervention. We need to talk to people to find out what happened next and reflect upon our findings in service of ongoing continuous improvement.

A word on 70:20:10

What, if anything, is different about this kind of approach and an approach informed by the now familiar 70:20:10 model of learning and development (Lombardo and Eichinger, 1996)? The 70:20:10 model is based on this finding: managers say that they learn 70 per cent of their leadership lessons through on-the-job experience, 20 per cent from other people and 10 per cent from courses and reading. These ratios seem broadly consistent with the emerging change model, in that both models emphasize the importance of structuring learning around events.

The 70:20:10 ratio in itself doesn't provide explicit guidance on how to build effective interventions; it's an outcome measure. Many organizations have responded to these guidelines by requiring that employees frame their development plans with reference to 70:20:10. This means categorizing different developmental activities. Jennings (2013), for example, suggests that the 70 per cent represents learning through day-to-day tasks, the 20 per cent includes learning through coaches, mentors, colleagues and experts, and the 10 per cent is about attending structured courses and programmes. If we relate this to the ECM (see Figure 16.4), this is in effect saying that a development plan should consist of events and some kind of conversation about those events with other people. We can position lectures and articles as 'voicing' in this context, while conversations with coaches, mentors, colleagues and experts may be monologic or dialogic.

The 70:20:10 model appears useful in framing real-life work as the context in which learning occurs. This is consistent with the idea that learning how to lead more effectively amid complexity is about learning about oneself through doing and reflecting on that doing with others. Once we adopt that principle the ratios become less meaningful; indeed they may distract the learner from the importance of the dialogic process through which we evolve and adapt to our surroundings. Conversations with coaches may be monologic or dialogic. Workshops may be designed to be monologic or dialogic. Breaking down the leader's learning experience into categories may distract from attending to essential aspects of design and lead to building unnecessarily fragmented solutions.

FIGURE 16.4 The emerging change model and 70:20:10

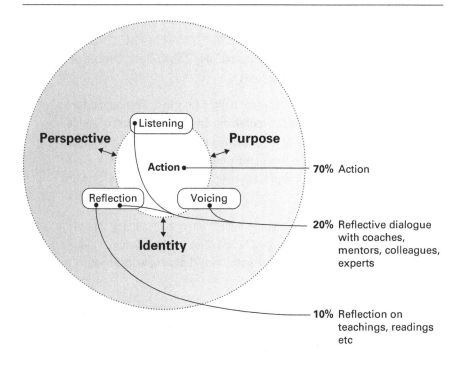

KEY POINTS

- The traditional approach to building capability is to focus on the development of individuals.

- This non-systemic approach often fails to deliver hoped-for outcomes, because programme designs fail to acknowledge the significance of reflective dialogue in facilitating change, and because the role of the prevailing organizational system in defining models of leadership is neither acknowledged nor managed.

- The effective practitioner adopts a more holistic perspective, looking for opportunities to leverage existing dialogue and facilitate more dialogue in the way that people go about business-as-usual.

- To manage change more effectively organizations need to become more authentic. This means providing individuals, teams and groups with new experiences and the opportunity to reflect upon those experiences together.

- Because meaning-making is a social process, leadership development interventions of the future will likely focus on team and group work. Workshop learning is more likely to be explicitly framed as a social learning process.

- Effective group learning interventions have a clear purpose, are subject to an ongoing evaluation strategy, are underpinned by reflective dialogue, and encourage systemic thinking.

- 70:20:10 models may broadly reflect how people spend their time learning when real-life experience is positioned as the primary locus for learning. Such models in themselves don't provide guidance on how to design effective processes.

The role of coaching

17

Reflective dialogue sits at the heart of change. The effective change leader is able to hold her perspective while simultaneously exploring the views of others. She is courageous, unafraid of articulating her own perspective, and able to express it in a way that takes into account what others are thinking and how they are feeling.

Building the capability of an organization to be able to engage in reflective dialogue takes time, and in Chapter 16 I suggested that one role of the effective change agent is to initiate and role-model this kind of dialogue as part of a broader ongoing development strategy. It's in this context that I want to place coaching, because coaching to me is precisely that – systemic reflective dialogue. Others define coaching differently such that its potential value as part of an effective change initiative is usually overlooked.

What is coaching?

There are multiple definitions of coaching. Some sit comfortably within a linear, sequential approach to change in which the 'coach' is the expert. The emphasis is on monologue:

> An effective coaching system [is one in which] managers review recent performance, evaluate it, and provide guidance, suggestions, and recommendations for improvement. (Lindbom, 2007)

> [Coaching is] providing timely guidance and feedback to help others strengthen specific knowledge/skill areas needed to accomplish a task or solve a problem. (Development Dimensions International)

Other definitions place more emphasis on helping people to work out solutions for themselves:

Coaching is the art of facilitating the unleashing of people's potential to reach meaningful, important objectives. (Rosinski, 2011)

Coaching is unlocking a person's potential to maximize their own performance. It is helping them to learn rather than teaching them. (Whitmore, 2002)

We see this dichotomy in the case study in Chapter 13, where an organization's collective definition of coaching begins as monologic and becomes more dialogic over time. We also see it in the approaches adopted by professional coaches. Some professional coaches, for example, emphasize the value of their personal experience in the corporate world, offering to share that experience with others. Other coaches emphasize listening and providing a safe space for executives to speak freely. Some role-model *all* aspects of reflective dialogue, including listening, providing open feedback, and creating a space for reflection. These are the coaches who would agree with Hawkins (2012) that dialogue sits at the heart of coaching.

I've recently been speaking to HR directors and OD managers across Australia, most of whom deploy external coaches in their business. I asked them about change and about coaching, and how change and coaching are linked. Talking about change, most spoke about the challenge of engaging the wider organization in the need for change, and the focus that leaders tend to have on telling people what needs to happen rather than engaging them in dialogue. On coaching, most talked about the role of the coach (internal or external) being to help people develop a greater sense of self-awareness in service of becoming more effective as a leader. When I asked about the link between coaching and change, many spoke specifically about the role of the external executive coach and the coach's capacity to help individuals to manage their part of the change process. A few spoke about the coach's role in working with groups and teams and only one or two suggested that coaching as a discipline is pretty much the same thing as reflective dialogue. For example, one person said:

Coaching is a conversation about stuff. It's about understanding the other party, listening, asking questions. It's getting them to think. One could argue that the stuff that leaders need to do in engaging people – we can call that coaching.

Another said:

The personal transformation required in change can *only* be facilitated by coaching. Coaching skills are critical in managing change. Creating insight and awareness is what's required to transition into a new state. Coaching is it.

From this perspective the capacity to engage in the kind of reflective dialogue required to facilitate change at the organizational level *is* coaching, yet it is rarely recognized as such. I think this may be because of some of the assumptions underpinning contemporary thinking about coaching may get in the way of its effectiveness in facilitating widespread change. These are assumptions about the individualistic nature of coaching, the way that coaching definitions often overemphasize the relative importance of listening, and the way that coaching is often defined in quite linear terms.

Assumption 1: Coaching is individualistic

Coaching in the organization has traditionally been individualistic. Executive coaching was widely used in its early days as an intervention to address problem behaviours (Bluckert, 2005). It was remedial in nature, with a focus on helping individuals conform to the expectations of their colleagues. Many early practitioners were counsellors seeking to extend their one-to-one work in a therapeutic context into the corporate domain. While coaching may no longer be used primarily as a remedial device, it is still used mainly as an individualistic intervention. Clutterbuck and Megginson (2005) go so far as to suggest that: 'Coaches, with their emphasis on one-to-one relationships, are a bit like sociable teenagers. They can focus obsessively on a relationship and pay precious little attention to the wider society.'

I don't think Clutterbuck and Megginson are suggesting that one-to-one coaching isn't useful; rather I suspect they are commenting on the mindset of the external practitioner. Lawrence and Whyte (2014) found that many practising coaches find it challenging to work with other stakeholders in the organization. Many talked about how 'tricky' it could be to manage the conflicting needs of their coachee and the paying client. Some described it as a 'balancing act'. Most said they handle that tension by seeking to establish expectations up-front with all parties. Only a minority said they check with the organization on an ongoing basis, and one coach said he did his best to avoid having conversations with the organization at all. Many leveraged boundaries on confidentiality to limit their interactions with other stakeholders as much as possible.

The individual focus of coaching sits well with traditional approaches to organizational development (OD) outlined in Chapter 14. The primary focus of the classical OD practitioner is on the individual so it's not surprising that the traditional OD practitioner values an essentially individualistic approach to coaching.

Assumption 2: Coaches ask questions and don't offer advice

In the world of executive coaching, giving a coachee advice is a no-no. For example: 'Non-directive coaching is, again, just that. You do not direct, instruct or tell' (Downey, 2003). Some coaches are likely to label those who do give advice as 'mentors': 'Mentors give advice and expert recommendations... Mentors talk about their own personal experiences, assuming it is relevant for the mentees' (Rosinski, 2003). Not surprisingly perhaps, mentors don't all agree with this distinction: 'It is the holistic nature of the mentoring role that distinguishes it from other learning or supporting roles, such as coaching... The mentor provides a very different kind of support – one based on reflective learning' (Clutterbuck, 2004).

As a coach myself I don't find the distinction between coaching and mentoring useful. I'm reminded of one of my coachees who came to me worried that his team's engagement scores had taken a sudden nose-dive. The scores had always been high, until this last survey. Worried, he conducted focus groups to work out what was going on and narrowed the issue down to one particular sub-team. Upon further enquiry he discovered that the leader of that team had just been on a coaching skills course and been told only to ask questions and to never give answers. So she adopted this as a new behaviour and whenever people popped their heads into her office asking for a quick piece of advice they found themselves frustrated. One of her reports spoke of a recurring dream in which he shoved a pencil up each of her nostrils every time she asked him a question. As Cavanagh (2006) says: 'Effective coaches often do tell. They educate their clients. They share their mental models, and tell them things when the answer eludes the client... The coach's telling is timely, the questions genuinely curious.'

I suspect the distinction between asking questions and giving answers reflects the relationship between coaching as a youngish discipline, and the prevalent monologic nature of communication within most organizations today. Most of us find it particularly challenging to put aside our own experiences and beliefs and to listen to others agenda-less. It is easy to give way to the little voices in our head telling us we know the answer and to provide those answers to the other person with all good intention. The rigid parameters that have been constructed around coaching may reflect that tension. However, if the coach is most useful when engaging in reflective dialogue then that must include voicing as well as listening. otherwise coaching runs the risk of becoming irrelevant. One of our storytellers, an HR director, was dismissive of the value of coaching: 'I think of coaching like a gym membership; as a place to go and vent in private.' The systemic coach listens, voices *and* facilitates reflection.

Assumption 3: Coaching is a linear sequential process

Perhaps the best known coaching model is the GROW model (Grant, 2012), popularized by Sir John Whitmore. GROW is an acronym that stands for Goals, Reality, Options, Way forward and many coaches base their practice on the model (Clutterbuck, 2010). The GROW model is in effect a framework for structuring a coaching conversation.

First the coach encourages the coachee to decide what she wants to achieve from the coaching – what is her goal (G). For example, the coachee may decide she wants her team to be more motivated and engaged. The coach works with the coachee to make the goal specific and measurable, with clear milestones for delivery (a 'SMART' goal). For example, the coachee might decide that she wants her team to be among the top 10 per cent of teams in the company, as measured by the next annual internal staff engagement survey.

Once the goal has been agreed, the coach encourages the coachee to ponder on the reality (R) of the current situation, and to identify what areas to best focus on. For example, this coachee did some homework and discovered that to get into the top 10 per cent the team's overall engagement score needed to increase from 66 to 82 per cent. The last survey showed the team felt they understood how their work contributed to the greater whole, and felt they were involved in decision making. The team scored low on the extent to which they felt they enjoyed a work–life balance and on the extent to which they felt members of the team trusted each other and worked together collaboratively.

The coach then encourages the coachee to come up with some options (O) as to what she might do moving forward. In this example the coachee might think about these five options:

1 Seeking extra resources.
2 Pushing back on team workload.
3 Diarizing fortnightly meetings with each of her staff to help them prioritize their work.
4 Removing a particular team member.
5 Engaging an external facilitator to run a team-building session.

The coach then asks the coachee to commit to what she will (W) do next, or the Way forward. In this case the coachee commits to actioning options 3 and 5 within the next fortnight.

As a coach I personally find the GROW model useful, but not when used linearly. Some coaches do apparently use it as if it were a step-by-step process. Clutterbuck (2010) tells the following story:

One of my 'favourite' ghastly examples is the coach who corralled the client into articulating a goal, then ploughed relentlessly on into the R of GROW until the client stopped the conversation, paused and said, 'Actually, my real issue is that I don't feel I have a purpose in my life anymore.' The coach nodded sympathetically. 'That's really interesting. I wish we had time to explore that. But let's park it and focus on the issue we started with…' In his reflection notes, the coach was blissfully unaware that this might not have been an appropriate response – he had followed the model.

Here again we see an example of a linear model being used to manage a complex situation. Even where the coach doesn't stick so dogmatically to the model, many coaches still place primary importance upon the early landing of a goal. I have been told by some clients that they expect the external coaches they deploy to make sure their coachees come up with goals early in the process, and ensure that the coachee is demonstrating some form of behavioural change within two or three sessions. If this doesn't happen, they say, they terminate the assignment. Clutterbuck (2010) suggests that some coaches seek to pin coachees down to specific goals at the beginning of an assignment in order to make life easier for themselves. I've witnessed many times in coaching skills classes, leaders declare their intention to listen and take their time to help the other person decide what's most important to them. So many find it hard to resist the temptation to step in and tell the other person what they think they should be working on.

A determination to ensure goals are formed early is entirely understandable. Most organizations are focused on getting things done. It's not difficult to empathize with a belief that the sooner goals are nailed down the sooner the goal will be achieved. The problem is that seeking to nail people down to their goals too early often makes it *less* likely those goals will be achieved (Clutterbuck, 2008). Again, we have a parallel with leading change, where to land the vision too early, without engaging in dialogue with others, may mean the vision is unlikely to be realized.

Systemic coaching

I use the term 'systemic coaching' only to highlight some of these critical assumptions about coaching. Systemic coaching doesn't constitute a particular set of skills or a particular discipline; it is a philosophy shared by some coaches and not by others, both external coaches and leaders engaged in reflective dialogue. If I'm seeking to use external coaches as part of my overall strategy for enhancing the capability of my organization, I may want to be able to differentiate between 'systemic' coaches and others, because not all coaches are systemic. Indeed relatively few coaches appear to be systemic in the way it is being defined here.

Few definitions of coaching include explicit reference to thinking systemically. In the external coaching world, thinking systemically seems to be the role of the coaching supervisor (Bachkirova *et al*, 2011; Hawkins and Schwenk, 2011). Gray and Jackson (2011) suggest that the role of the coaching supervisor is, specifically, to handle tensions between coach, coachee and organization. Why is the systemic perspective flagged as an attribute of an effective coaching supervisor, but not a coach *per se*? It appears this may be a temporal phenomenon reflecting where coaching is at today as a discipline. The challenge remains then: how to identify the 'systemic' coach.

First, the systemic coach may not describe herself as a coach at all. Grant *et al* (2010) suggest that coaching may be usefully defined specifically as an individualistic intervention, and that working with teams and organizations may be considered to be the domain of organizational development and HR professionals. Certainly it's true that many coaches who specialize in individual work seek to minimize their interactions with other stakeholders and some feel uncomfortable working in team/group settings. On the other hand I suspect the 'systemic coach' finds herself inevitably drawn to working with teams and organizations, curious to understand better and play a role in the wider context within which individual coachees are operating. As Cavanagh (2006) puts it: 'Coaching from a complex adaptive systems perspective does not draw a dichotomy between the individual and the team. Rather, working with an individual is working with the team/wider organization.'

The 'systemic coach' may well describe herself as a facilitator or a consultant. Here again, as we did with words like 'communication' and 'listening', we may need to navigate the sea of assumptions and beliefs that underpin our current use of language.

The systemic coach is comfortable voicing a view or offering an opinion when it feels appropriate. The systemic coach recognizes that to withhold a view or to refrain from giving feedback may not help coachees achieve their goals. It may feel inauthentic to withhold those views from the dialogue. On the other hand the systemic coach is constantly mindful of the purpose of coaching: to facilitate a reflective process rather than directly provide guidance and advice, and is alert to the possibility that providing a perspective may either facilitate or interrupt that process depending on how and when it is delivered.

The systemic coach is nimble, and can articulate a strategy for managing the different demands of stakeholders without breaching parameters of confidentiality. The systemic coach sees the organization through a wide angle lens and recognizes her own role in the emergence of change. The coach isn't a neutral onlooker. As soon as the coach opens her mouth in the presence of another, she understands she has become a part of the system. Simply by expressing a view, the coach begins to play a role in the surfacing and clarification of different perspectives and the emergence of new possibilities. The systemic coach recognizes her role in the process of change and is comfortable in the dialogic space. This is in contrast to the coach who feels less nimble in this space, and so limits her interactions so as not to betray confidentialities. The systemic coach is constantly mindful of her role in the process, as someone who is paid by the organization to work with an individual or teams. Rather than think in terms of trade-offs between the individual or team's needs and the needs of the organization, the systemic coach is always thinking how best to act in a way that is in service of all.

Each of these aspects of the 'systemic coach' comes down to mindset, a systemic perspective on the nature of the work and a belief in the significance of authentic reflective dialogue. In other words the same 'fearless curiosity' we have already identified as characterizing an effective change leader.

Systemic coaching at work

Because coaching is often conducted in private and bounded by walls of confidentiality, it is often shrouded in a veil of secrecy, with coach, coachee and client co-creating a scenario in which the coaching conversation is regarded as not discussable. Many published studies on coaching have focused on outcomes without necessarily providing much insights into how coaching works. Evidence exists, for example, that coaching has significant positive effects on performance, attitudes, resilience, wellbeing and self-regulation (Theebom *et al*, 2013), but how?

Stacey (2012) distinguishes between 'instrumentally rational, step-following' forms of coaching, and coaching as what he calls 'work therapy', suggesting that the latter approach is more likely to be useful in facilitating change than the former. More specifically he suggests that the potential contribution of a coach is to encourage the development of 'exploratory reflexivity'. According to the dictionary, 'reflexivity' refers to circular relationships between cause and effect. In other words, it is a view of the world that is more complex than A causes B; it is a world in which A and B affect each other. What Stacey appears to be saying is that coaching is useful in helping people explore how things impact on each other. Is this what happens in coaching?

Over the last few years I've led a series of studies into what actually happens in individual coaching assignments. This research was conducted within a coaching organization whose coaches, broadly speaking, see their role as being to facilitate change rather than to direct their coachees and tell them what they should be doing. In a recent study I spoke to 53 people who had been coached over a period of more than five years. I found that people coached five years ago, or longer, said that the impact of coaching still endured. I also asked people if coaching had changed the way they operate at times of change. Seventy-seven per cent of people said it had, describing the impact in terms of self-awareness, reflection, confidence, relationships and seeing the bigger picture.

1. Self-awareness

People talked about becoming more aware about how they think, how they do things and how to better manage their emotions. People came out of coaching with an enhanced sense of who they were and how they operated. For example, one person said:

> It helped me realize you can't automatically change. It helps to consciously manage that change. It's not as straightforward as I thought; you need to manage the change in yourself. We don't often think about that.

2. Reflection

People specifically called out reflection as the means by which they came to attain greater insights about themselves. For example:

> He got me to think about why I do things; he made me reflective. Reflection has become routine now. He always challenged me very positively.

3. Confidence

Some people explicitly mentioned how reflection helped them deal with change by helping them to feel more confident. For example:

> I was in an invidious position which was very difficult to deal with. I would have walked otherwise, but the coaching helped me put things into perspective and I'm now more powerful about making a stand for myself.

4. Relationships

People talked about paying more attention to other's perspectives, being open to those perspectives, asking more questions and listening. For example:

> Yes, I try and communicate more, to touch base with people. I ask more questions. I try to be open and listening rather than closed and directive.

5. Seeing the bigger picture

People talked about having developed an enhanced capacity to stand back and see the bigger picture. For example:

> I have more foresight in terms of the impact of change. I take a step back and think what will happen long term.

Systemic coaching would therefore appear to work not only as a process by which to help others navigate change in the moment, but as a process that leaves others more capable of navigating change in the future. Participation in reflective dialogue helps us to recognize the value of reflective dialogue such so we are able to take that practice and build it into our own way of leading.

Coaching culture/change culture

Many organizations set out to build coaching cultures. I recounted the story of one such company in Chapter 13. Quite what a 'coaching culture' means, of course, depends on how coaching is defined. If we define coaching in terms of providing people with advice and guidance on how they could best perform their role, then a coaching culture might look like a lot of expert managers paying attention to the quality of work being produced by people in their team and intervening where necessary to help them deliver better outcomes. Leading change in such a culture may prove challenging since the prevailing form of interaction is monologue.

If, on the other hand, we take a systemic coaching perspective then we are attempting to build a culture in which people are constantly attuned to the connections between people and things when trying to get things done. We are attempting to build a culture in which people are encouraged to become more self-aware and authentic, in which people pay attention to each other and are curious about each other's beliefs and values. In other words we are attempting to build a culture in which people know how to change together: a change culture.

If the experience of being coached by a systemic coach helps people to think more systemically, then bringing such coaches into an organization makes sense strategically. However, the world is complex, and we shouldn't expect that the task of building a change culture will be so simple. Clutterbuck and Megginson (2005) and Cooper (2011) point out that introducing coaching and coaching skills programmes is unlikely in itself to stimulate an immediate transition into such a culture. Indeed Clutterbuck and Megginson (2005) suggest that one-off coaching training initiatives tend to distract attention from broader aspects of cultural change. From the perspective of the ECM we would expect nothing else. To enhance the capability of the organization to effect change means encouraging leaders and managers to go about doing things differently; it requires a systemic approach to building internal capability over time.

KEY POINTS

- People define 'coaching' in many different ways. Some define it as a relationship between two people, in which the coach may listen but not tell, structured on a sequential process. Others see their role in terms of facilitating reflective dialogue, including listening, voicing and meaning-making.

- The systemic coach is comfortable working with individuals, groups and teams. She is able to hold the needs of the organization alongside the needs of the people she is coaching and evaluates her contribution in terms of the impact she has on the organization as a whole.

- Systemic coaching is therefore the practice of systemic reflective dialogue. In putting together strategies to build organizational capability the internal practitioner may choose to consider the strategic deployment of external systemic coaches and the cultivation of an internal 'coaching' mindset.

REFERENCES

Allen, J, Jimmieson, N L, Bordia, P and Irmer, B E (2007) Uncertainty during organizational change: managing perceptions through communication, *Journal of Change Management*, 7 (2), pp 187–210

Ansoff, H I (1991) Critique of Henry Mintzberg's 'The Design School: reconsidering the basic premises of strategic management', *Strategic Management Journal*, 12, pp 449–61

Argyris, C (1991) Teaching smart people how to learn, *Harvard Business Review*, 69 (3), pp 99–109

Arthur, W A, Bennett, W, Edens, P S and Bell, S T (2003) Effectiveness of training in organizations: a meta-analysis of design and evaluation features, *Journal of Applied Psychology*, 88 (2), pp 234–45

Avolio, B J and Gardner, W L (2005) Authentic leadership development: getting to the root of positive forms of leadership, *The Leadership Quarterly*, 16, pp 315–38

Bachkirova, T, Jackson, P and Clutterbuck, D (2011) *Coaching and Mentoring Supervision Theory and Practice*, Open University Press, McGraw-Hill, Maidenhead

Beech, N, Kajzer-Mitchell, I, Oswick, C and Saren, M (2011) Barriers to change and identity work in the swampy lowland, *Journal of Change Management*, 11 (3), pp 289–304

Beisser, A (1970) The paradoxical theory of change, in (eds) J Fagan and I Lee Shepherd, *Gestalt Therapy Now*, pp 77–80, HarperCollins, New York

Bluckert, P (2005) Critical factors in executive coaching – the coaching relationship, *Industrial and Commercial Training*, 37 (7), pp 336–40

Bohm, D (1996) *On Dialogue*, Routledge, London

Boje, D M (2012) Reflections: what does quantum physics of storytelling mean for change management? *Journal of Change Management*, 12 (3), pp 253–71

Bond, C and Seneque, M (2012) Exploring organizational identity in the context of transformational change: a South African case study, *Journal of Change Management*, 12 (1), pp 13–30

Burke, R J and Cooper, C L (2000) *The Organization in Crisis*, Blackwell, Oxford

Burnes, B (2004) Kurt Lewin and complexity theories: back to the future? *Journal of Change Management*, 4 (4), pp 309–25

Burnes, B (2011) Introduction: why does change fail, and what can we do about it? *Journal of Change Management*, 11 (4), pp 445–50

Cavanagh, M (2006) Coaching from a systemic perspective: a complex adaptive conversation, in (eds) D R Stober and A M Grant, *Evidence based Coaching*

Handbook: Putting best practices to work for your clients, pp 313–54, John Wiley, New Jersey

Charan, R and Colvin, G (1999) Why CEOs fail, *Fortune*, June 21, pp 68–78

Clutterbuck, D (2004) *Everyone Needs a Mentor: Fostering talent in your organisation*, 4th edn, CIPD, London

Clutterbuck, D (2008) What's happening in coaching and mentoring? And what is the difference between them? *Development and Learning in Organizations*, **22** (4), pp 8–10

Clutterbuck, D (2010) Coaching reflection: the liberated coach, *Coaching: An International Journal of Theory, Research and Practice*, **3** (1), pp 73–81

Clutterbuck, D and Megginson, D (2005) *Making Coaching Work: Creating a coaching culture*, CIPD, London

Conway, E and Monks, K (2011) Change from below: the role of middle managers in mediating paradoxical change, *Human Resource Management Journal*, **21** (2), pp 190–203

Cooper, J (2011) The practice of coaching by managers: impacts of organizational, cultural, and other supports and hindrances, *International Journal of Coaching in Organizations*, **30**, 8 (2), pp 74–85

Corbin, J and Strauss, A (1990) Grounded theory research: procedures, canons and evaluative criteria, *Zeitschrift fur Soziologie*, **19** (6), pp 418–27

Covey, S R (1989) *Seven Habits of Highly Effective People*, Simon & Schuster, New York

Development Dimensions International, https://www.ddiworld.com/DDIWorld/media/learning-links/learningandassessmentlinks_competencylinks_br_ddi.pdf?ext=.pdf

Downey, M (2003) *Effective Coaching: Lessons from the coach's coach*, 2nd edn, Texere, London

Duck, J D (1998) Managing change: the art of balancing, *Harvard Business Review*, **71** (6), pp 109–18

Eckert, R, Ekelund, B Z, Gentry, W A and Dawson, J F (2010) I don't see me like you see me, but is that a problem? Cultural influences on rating discrepancy in 360-degree feedback instruments, *European Journal of Work and Organizational Psychology*, **19** (3), pp 259–78

Ford, J D and Ford, L W (2010) Stop blaming resistance to change and start using it, *Organizational Dynamics*, **39** (1), pp 24–36

Ford, J D, Ford, L W and D'Amelio, A (2008) Resistance to change: the rest of the story, *Academy of Management Review*, **33** (2), pp 362–77

Frankl, V E (2004) *Man's Search for Meaning*, Rider, London

Garavan, T N, Morley, M and Flynn, M (1997) 360 degree feedback: its role in employee development, *Journal of Management Development*, **16** (2), pp 134–47

Garvey Berger, J (2006) [accessed 29 April 2014] Key concepts for understanding the work of Robert Kegan, Kenning Associates, tinyurl.com/khvyndh

Garvey Berger, J (2012) *Changing on the Job*, Stanford Business Books, Stanford, CA

Gover, L and Duxbury, L (2012) Organizational Faultlines: social identity dynamics and organizational change, *Journal of Change Management*, **12** (1), pp 53–75

Grant, A M (2012) An integrated model of goal-focused coaching: an evidence-based framework for teaching and practice, *International Coaching Psychology Review*, **7** (2), pp 146–65

Grant, A M, Cavanagh, M J, Parker, H M and Passmore, J (2010) The state of play in coaching today: a comprehensive review of the field, in (eds) G P Hodgkinson and J K Ford, *International Review of Industrial and Organizational Psychology*, pp 125–65, John Wiley, New Jersey

Gray, D E and Jackson, P (2011) Coaching supervision in the historical context of psychotherapeutic and counselling models: a meta-model, in (eds) T Bachkirova, P Jackson and D Clutterbuck, *Coaching and Mentoring Supervision Theory and Practice,* pp 15–27, Open University Press, McGraw-Hill, Maidenhead

Hawkins, P (2012) *Creating a Coaching Culture*, McGraw-Hill, Maidenhead

Hawkins, P and Schwenk, N (2011) The seven-eyed model of coaching supervision, in (eds) T Bachkirova, P Jackson and D Clutterbuck, *Coaching and Mentoring Supervision Theory and Practice,* pp 28–40, Open University Press, McGraw-Hill, Maidenhead

Heifetz, R A (1994) *Leadership Without Easy Answers*, Belknap Harvard, Cambridge, MA

Higgs, M and Rowland, D (2005) All changes great and small: exploring approaches to change and its leadership, *Journal of Change Management*, **5** (2), pp 121–51

Higgs, M and Rowland, D (2010): Emperors With clothes on: the role of self-awareness in developing effective change leadership, *Journal of Change Management*, **10** (4), pp 369–85

Hogg, M and Terry, D (2000) Social identity and self-categorization processes in organizational contexts, *Academy of Management Review*, **25** (1), pp 121–40

Hughes, M (2011) Do 70 per cent of all organizational change initiatives really fail? *Journal of Change Management*, **11** (4), pp 451–64

Isaacs, W (1999) *Dialogue and the Art of Thinking Together*, Currency Doubleday, New York

Jabri, M, Adrian, A D and Boje, D (2008) Reconsidering the role of conversations in change communication: a contribution based on Bakhtin, *Journal of Organizational Change Management*, **21** (6), pp 667–85

Jackman, J J and Strober, M H (2003) Fear of feedback, *Harvard Business Review*, **81** (4), pp 101–7

Jennings, M (2013) [accessed 29 April 2014] Ten 70:20:10 FAQs, 70 20 10 Forum https://www.702010forum.com/Posts/view/guidance-ten-common-70-20-10-faqs-1

Johansson, C and Heide, M (2008) Speaking of change: three communication approaches in studies of organizational change, *Corporate Communications: An International Journal*, **13** (3), pp 288–305

Judge, W and Douglas, T (2009) Organizational change capacity: the systematic development of a scale, *Journal of Organizational Change Management*, **22** (6), pp 635–49

Jung, C G (1933) *Modern Man in Search of a Soul*, Kegan Paul, London

Kahane, A (2008) *Solving Tough Problems: An open way of talking, listening and creating new realities*, 2nd edn, Berrett-Koehler Publishers, San Francisco, CA

Kantor, D (2012) *Reading the Room*, Jossey-Bass, San Francisco, CA

Kaplan, R S and Norton, D P (2000) Having trouble with your strategy? Then map it, *Harvard Business Review*, **78** (5), pp 167–76

Kegan, R (1994) *In Over our Heads: The mental demands of modern life*, Harvard University Press, Cambridge, MA

Kernis, M H (2003) Toward a conceptualization of optimal self-esteem, *Psychological Inquiry*, **14**, pp 1–26

Kotter, J P (1995) Leading change: Why transformation efforts fail, *Harvard Business Review*, **73** (2), pp 59–67

Larkin, T, and Larkin, S (1994) *Communicating Change*, McGraw-Hill, New York

Lawrence, P and Whyte, A (2014) What is coaching supervision and is it important? *Coaching: An International Journal of Theory, Research and Practice*, **7** (1), pp 39–55

Lewin, K (1951) *Field Theory in Social Science*, Harper & Row, New York

Lewis, L K, Schmisseir, A M, Stephens, K K and Weir, K E (2006) Advice on communicating during organizational change, *Journal of Business Communication*, **43** (2), pp 113–37

Lindbom, D (2007) A culture of coaching: the challenge of managing performance for long-term results, *Organization Development Journal*, **25** (2), pp 101–6

Litchenstein, B M (1996) Evolution or transformation: a critique and alternative to punctuated equilibrium, in (ed) D Moore, *Academy of Management Best Paper Proceedings*, pp 291–5, Academy of Management, Vancouver

Lombardo, M M and Eichinger, R W (1996) *The Career Architect Development Planner*, Lominger, Minneapolis

McCann, L, Hassard, J and Morris, J (2004) Middle managers, the new organizational ideology and corporate restructuring: comparing Japanese and Anglo-American management systems, *Competition and Change*, **8** (1), pp 27–44

McClellan, J (2011) Reconsidering communication and the discursive politics of organizational change, *Journal of Change Management*, **11** (4), pp 465–80

McKee, R (1999) *Story*, Methuen, London

Marshak, R M and Grant, D (2008) Organizational discourse and new organization development practices, *British Journal of Management*, **19**, pp S7–S19

Michaelis, B, Stegmaier, R and Sonntag, K (2009) Affective commitment to change and innovation implementation behavior: the role of charismatic leadership and employees' trust in top management, *Journal of Change Management*, 9 (4), pp 399–417

Mintzberg, H (1990) The design school: reconsidering the basic premises of strategic management, *Strategic Management Journal*, 11 (3), pp 171–95

Mitchell, R K, Agle, B R and Wood, D J (1997) Toward a theory of stakeholder identification and salience: defining the principle of who and what really counts, *The Academy of Management Review*, 22 (4), pp 853–86

Piderit, S K (2000) Rethinking resistance and recognizing ambivalence: a multidimensional view of attitudes toward an organizational change, *Academy of Management Review*, 25, pp 783–94

Raelin, J D and Cataldo, C G (2011) Whither middle management? Empowering interface and the failure of organizational change, *Journal of Change Management*, 11 (4), pp 481–507

Reissner, S C (2010), Change, meaning and identity at the workplace, *Journal of Organizational Change Management*, 23 (3), pp 287–99

Rodgers, C (2007) *Informal coalitions: Mastering the hidden dynamics of organizational change*, Palgrave Macmillan, Basingstoke

Rosinski, P (2003) *Coaching Across Cultures: New tools for leveraging national, corporate and professional differences*, Nicholas Brealey, London

Rosinski, P (2011) Global coaching for organizational development, *International Journal of Coaching in Organizations*, 30, 8 (2), pp 45–66

Sammut-Bonnici, R and Wensley, R (2002) Darwinism, probability and complexity: market-based organisational transformation and change explained through the theories of evolution, *International Journal of Management Reviews*, 4 (3), pp 291–315

Sargut, G and McGrath, R G (2011) Learning to live with complexity, *Harvard Business Review*, 89 (9), pp 68–76

Scase, R and Goffee, R (1986) Are the rewards worth the effort? Changing managerial values in the 1980s, *Personnel Review*, 15 (4), pp 3–6

Scase, R and Goffee, R (1989) *Reluctant Managers: Their work and lifestyles*, Unwin Hyman, London

Schön, D A (1991) *The Reflective Practitioner*, Ashgate, Farnborough

Senge *et al* (1994) *The Fifth Discipline Fieldbook*, Currency Doubleday, New York

Shaw, P (1997) Intervening in the shadow systems of organizations: consulting from a complexity perspective, *Journal of Organizational Change Management*, 10 (3), pp 235–50

Shaw, P (2002) *Changing Conversations in Organizations: A complexity approach to change (Complexity and emergence in organizations)*, Routledge, London

Smollan, R K and Sayers, J G (2009) Organizational culture, change and emotions: a qualitative study, *Journal of Change Management*, 9 (4), pp 435–57

Stacey, R (2012) *Tools and Techniques of Leadership and Management: Meeting the challenge of complexity,* Routledge, London

Sullivan, T (2011) Embracing complexity. An interview with Michael J Mauboussin, *Harvard Business Review,* **89** (9), pp 89–92

Theeboom, T, Beersma, B and van Vianen, A E M (2013) Does coaching work? A meta-analysis on the effects of coaching on individual level outcomes in an organizational context, *The Journal of Positive Psychology,* **9** (1), pp 1–118

Thomas, R and Hardy, C (2011) Reframing resistance to organizational change, *Scandinavian Journal of Management,* **27,** pp 322–31

Thomas, R and Linstead, A (2002) Losing the plot? Middle managers and identity, *Organization,* **9** (1), pp 71–93

Thurlow, A and Helms Mills, J (2009) Change, talk and sensemaking, *Journal of Organizational Change Management,* **22** (5), pp 459–79

Treacy, M and Wiersma, F (1996) *The Discipline of Market Leaders,* Harper Collins, London

Trilling, L (1972) *Sincerity and Authenticity,* Harvard University Press, Cambridge, MA

Tsoukas, H (2009) A dialogical approach to the creation of new knowledge in organizations, *Organizational Science,* **20** (6), pp 941–57

Tsoukas, H and Chia, R (2002) On organizational becoming, *Organization Science,* **13** (5), pp 567–82

Tsoukas, H and Hatch, M J (2001) Complex thinking, complex practice: the case for a narrative approach to organizational complexity, *Human Relations,* **54** (8), pp 979–1013

Turnbull, S (2001) Corporate ideology: Meanings and contradictions for middle managers, *British Journal of Management,* **12** (3), pp 231–42

van de Ven, A H and Sun, K (2011) Breakdowns in implementing models of organization change, *Academy of Management Perspectives,* **25** (3), pp 58–74

van der Heijden, B I J M and Nijhof, A H J (2004) The value of subjectivity: problems and prospects for 360-degree appraisal systems, *The International Journal of Human Resource Management,* **15** (3), pp 493–511

van Dijk, R and van Dick, R (2009) Navigating organizational change: change leaders, employee resistance and work-based identities, *Journal of Change Management,* **9** (2), pp 143–63

van Vuuren, M and Elving, W J L (2008) Practical implications and a research agenda for communicating organizational change, *Corporate Communications: An International Journal,* **13** (3), pp 349–59

Watson, J D (1968) *The Double Helix: A personal account of the discovery of the structure of DNA,* Weidenfeld and Nicolson, London

Weick, K E (2011) Reflections: change agents as change poets on reconnecting flux and hunches, *Journal of Change Management,* **11** (1), pp 7–20

Weick, K E, Sutcliffe, K M and Obstfeld, D (2005) Organizing and the process of sensemaking, *Organization Science*, **16** (4), pp 409–21

Werkman, R (2010) Reinventing organization development: how a sensemaking perspective can enrich OD theories and interventions, *Journal of Change Management*, **10** (4), pp 421–38

Whitmore, J (2002) *Coaching for Performance*, 3rd edn, Nicholas Brealey, London

INDEX

Page numbers in *italics* denote information contained within a figure or table.

CPSIA information can be obtained at www.ICGtesting.com
Printed in the USA
LVOW05s1457161214

419118LV00005B/128/P

9 780749 471682